FROM FACELESS
TO LEGENDARY

FOR COACHES,
MENTORS, TRAINERS,
AND CONSULTANTS

To Francesca:
Be Legendary!

ANDREI MINCOV

FROM FACELESS TO LEGENDARY

FOR COACHES, MENTORS, TRAINERS, AND CONSULTANTS

THE ULTIMATE INSIDER'S GUIDE TO INTELLECTUAL PROPERTY

From Faceless to Legendary for Coaches, Mentors, Trainers, and Consultants /
The Ultimate Insider's Guide to Intellectual Property /
Mincov, Andrei

ISBN-13: 978-1519572912
ISBN-10: 1519572912

Cover design: Andrei Mincov

Published by 10-10-10 Publishing
Markham, ON
Canada

ALSO BY ANDREI MINCOV

*The Ultimate Insider's Guide to Intellectual Property:
When to See an IP Lawyer and Ask Educated Questions About
Copyright, Trademarks, Patents, Trade Secrets,
Industrial Designs, Contracts, and Other Ways of
Protecting Your Ideas and Covering Your Assets*®

http://IPBook.ca

From Faceless to Legendary™:
*The Ultimate Insider's Guide to Intellectual Property
for Bars, Cafes, and Restaurants*

http://FacelessToLegendary.Com/Restaurants

GET ALL THE HELP YOU CAN GET

Order your free trademark search:
http://freeTMsearch.com

Get your brands trademarked:
http://TrademarkFactory.com

Watch cartoons explaining trademarks in plain English:
http://TrademarkCartoons.com

Buy contract templates related to intellectual property:
http://NiceContracts.com

Order Intellectual Property Strategy Review consultation:
http://IPStrategyReview.com

TABLE OF CONTENTS

FOREWORD
BY ADAM MARKEL

If there's one thing I've learned in my years of practicing law, developing successful businesses, and being a lead trainer and CEO for *Peak Potentials*® (recently rebranded as *New Peaks*™), it's that reaching your full potential is a **choice**. There's no secret shortcut or "special sauce" that makes it happen—it's just putting one foot in front of the other, one right thought in front of the next.

Now, I don't always like to dwell on it, but you and I both know that competition in the coaching industry is fierce. The world we live in is full of challenges. Knowing what those challenges are is critical to overcoming them, and it *always* pays to have help.

And if there's one person who understands the challenges that trainers, mentors, consultants, and coaches face when it comes to intellectual property, it's Andrei Mincov.

His bestseller, *The Ultimate Insider's Guide to Intellectual Property*™, introduced this sometimes intimidating subject to a general audience. He followed that up by launching the *From Faceless to Legendary*™ series of books on intellectual property designed to highlight how IP applies to specific industries.

The first book in the series showed the challenges and significant opportunities of trademark law and other areas of IP to bar, cafe, and restaurant owners.

You are holding the second book of the series, which speaks to *our* needs as coaches, trainers, mentors, and consultants—with clarity, focus, and humor.

I like to say that the first step to finding great things is to *expect* great things—and you're paging through something great right now.

Unlike some books you've read, you won't find yourself skipping over headings that don't apply to you, because they *all* do. Andrei *gets* it.

No matter where you are in your career—a seasoned veteran on the training circuit or someone just getting started—I can guarantee that intellectual property is *already* important to your livelihood.

If I could give you one piece of advice today, it's this: give Andrei Mincov's book *ten minutes* of your time, and you'll see how intellectual property can help unleash the true potential of your business. Andrei is an assured, engaging communicator who doesn't bog you down in "legalese"—and believe me, with 17 years as a practicing attorney, I've heard and used my share of *that*.

Andrei and I have a few things in common. For many years, we were both lawyers—until one day we realized that we could help a lot more people outside of our law offices. I became the CEO of *New Peaks*, and Andrei gave up his lawyer license to build his company, *Trademark Factory®*, into the only firm in the world that helps business owners like you register trademarks for a single all-inclusive flat fee, with a 100% money-back guarantee—something unheard of in the world of law firms.

In a way, Andrei's surrender of his law license marked his growth from being a lawyer who understands entrepreneurship to being an entrepreneur and a visionary with deep knowledge of intellectual property laws.

At Peaks, we don't endorse third-party services unless we've tried them ourselves. We eat our own cooking. When Andrei told me about *Trademark Factory®*'s unique approach to trademarking, as a former attorney, I was very surprised because lawyers are not exactly known for predictable fees and guarantees. But it made perfect sense to me as an entrepreneur. We chose Andrei's firm to file new trademark applications for my company—and we're very happy we did.

So what is it that makes Andrei's advice so relevant to the work *you* do?

Your brand, course content, and the proprietary behind-the-scenes secrets are all *your* intellectual property—and if you're not prepared to protect the essence of your business from unscrupulous copycats and aggressive competitors, you're doing yourself (and your students) a great disservice. The consequences can be devastating.

Trademark Factory®'s tagline is *If It's Worth Promoting, It's Worth Protecting*™. I couldn't agree more. If you spend time, money, and energy to build and promote your coaching business, you owe it to yourself to protect its most valuable assets. You also owe it to those who turn to you for advice.

As you spend more time with Andrei's book, you'll discover how truly successful trainers and coaches use intellectual property to expand their global reach. This book will not replace professional do-it-for-you services, but it will give you confidence and understanding to know when to seek such services to implement IP strategy for your business.

So do yourself a favor and *keep reading*. Learn how professionals like Andrei can help you protect the accomplishments you've already made and lay the groundwork for your future success. Make this moment count, listen to what Andrei has to say, and find out what it really means to go from *Faceless to Legendary!*

Adam Markel
CEO and Lead Trainer of *New Peaks*™
(formerly *Peak Potentials*®)
Author of the forthcoming book *Pivot*

INTRODUCTION:

WHY SHOULD COACHES, MENTORS, TRAINERS, AND CONSULTANTS CARE ABOUT INTELLECTUAL PROPERTY?

WHO IS THIS BOOK FOR?

As the title of this book suggests, it was written for coaches, mentors, trainers, and consultants.

As the author of the bestselling, 360-page book, *The Ultimate Insider's Guide to Intellectual Property*, and a former intellectual property lawyer with over twenty years of experience, I've met thousands of business owners who think that intellectual property might be very important for other industries, but is largely irrelevant for theirs.

The thing is, they view intellectual property as groundbreaking inventions owned by multi-billion-dollar transnational corporations. They think, *"I'm just a business coach, I don't need any of that!"*

While many of the ways that giants in other industries use intellectual property are indeed irrelevant to you, there is a time and place for making proper use of it in *your* business.

As a business owner myself, I know how frustrating it can be to read through pages and pages of information that may be useful for someone else, but is irrelevant to me.

From Faceless to Legendary: The Ultimate Insider's Guide to Intellectual Property for Coaches, Mentors, Trainers, and Consultants was not written to show you how much I know about intellectual property on an academic level. This book has nothing but practical advice that relates to *your* business as a coach, mentor, trainer, or consultant. Ignore it at your peril.

There are many words to refer to people that this book is for—coaches, business coaches, personal coaches, life coaches, success trainers, personal development leaders, mentors, gurus, consultants, speakers, presenters, mastermind facilitators, advisors, trainers, etc. I couldn't add all of these to the title of the book, but that does not mean this book is not for you.

If you are in the business of sharing your knowledge, skills and experience to help people and companies get better at what they do, this book is for you.

Throughout this book, I will use coaches, mentors, trainers, and consultants interchangeably. I know they are not the same, but trust me, you would get tired of reading about "your business as a coach, mentor, trainer, or consultant" very quickly if I didn't do this. So if you are a mentor and read about what coaches should do to protect their intellectual property, don't dismiss it. It has as much relevance for you as it does for a coach.

Finally, this book is not designed to turn you into a lawyer. It should not be considered legal advice. Even though it inevitably uses examples of laws from particular jurisdictions, it's not a textbook on Canadian or U.S. laws. This book is about *you* and *your coaching business* and how *you* can use intellectual property laws (wherever you are) to *protect your ideas and cover your assets*®.

I need to make this disclaimer to make sure we're on the same page. I have made every effort to make sure this book contains accurate and authoritative information about the subject matter covered. However, no warranties or guarantees are made that the information is or remains accurate or updated. This book is published for information purposes only. If you need legal advice, specific business advice, or require other assistance, seek the services of a competent professional. Neither I nor Trademark Factory International Inc. assume any responsibility or liability of any kind for whatever decisions you purportedly make as a result of something you read in this book. Even if you think your situation is the same as a situation described in this book, do not assume that you can rely on this book as legal advice.

WHAT IS IP?

While *intellectual property* sounds like a legal term, in fact, it is not. Intellectual property (usually abbreviated to *IP*) is merely an umbrella term for a number of different areas of law, each with its separate subject matter, rules, requirements, and scope.

> **Intellectual property is an umbrella term for a number of different areas of law.**

These areas of law are trademarks, copyright and neighbouring rights, patents, industrial designs, and trade secrets. Contracts and contractual rights also play an important role in how intellectual property is used, so they should also be included under the same umbrella.

Intellectual property is a convenient term that refers to a set of exclusive rights recognized by governments regarding various intangible assets created by the human mind. This includes brand names, logos, taglines, design, photographs, business processes, apps, customer lists, and all other rights resulting from intellectual activity in the industrial, scientific, literary, or artistic fields.

All of these rights may be grouped into two categories:

- the rights to use your own intellectual property without interference from others; and

- the rights to prevent others from using your intellectual property.

Importantly, the focus of intellectual property is on granting you an exclusive right to control the use of your IP by others. This includes preventing anybody from using your IP without your permission. This is about getting a competitive advantage over everyone who is not smart, creative, talented or industrious enough to have come up with whatever you came up with.

The only obligation your intellectual property rights impose on others is the obligation to not use it without your permission. Just because you own a trademark or a copyright is not sufficient to force others to buy a coaching session with you. But it *is* sufficient to prevent others from offering their coaching services under the same name or from stealing photographs from your website.

The reasoning behind intellectual property is simple: you have invested time, talent, money, and effort to create something that didn't exist before, so you should be able to preserve an advantage over everyone else who may be willing to steal what you have created.

You may have noticed that I stated intellectual property is about rights recognized by governments. This is important because intellectual property rights are independent from country to country. While there are several international treaties that facilitate international protection of IP, you have a separate set of rights protected under the laws of each country.

Make sure you understand these key points as you keep reading this book:

-   Intellectual property is not uniformly regulated under a single unified law;

-   Intellectual property is not about letting you use what you have created;

- Intellectual property is not about forcing others to use what you have created;

- Intellectual property is about giving you the right to prevent others from using what you created; and

- Intellectual property is protected on a per-country level.

FOCUS ON BOTH IP COMING IN AND IP GOING OUT

I hear it all the time. A trainer says, *"I really don't have anything to protect, the business is really just myself and my admin staff, I'm happy to share my experience with the world, so there's no reason why we need to talk to an intellectual property lawyer."*

Wrong. Just because you are not interested in protecting your own stuff, does not mean you can safely ignore the intellectual property rights owned by others. IP is a double-edged sword: think of it as intellectual property that comes IN your door and intellectual property that goes OUT your door—in that order.

> **Just because you're not interested in protecting your own intellectual property, does not mean you can safely ignore the IP of others.**

Intellectual property coming IN your door is what you create, what you have other people create for you, what you buy from other people, and what you steal from other people. And no, I'm not saying you should steal from other people, but if you're using someone else's photographs on your website without the photographer's permission, that's still intellectual property coming IN your door, albeit stolen.

Anything that you create or use can be viewed as coming IN your door, regardless of whether it comes in legally or illegally. Once you have a good understanding of what is coming IN your door, you can look at how to build an effective intellectual property strategy.

Intellectual property going OUT your door is even simpler to understand because this is what most people think about when they hear the words "intellectual property". This is commonly thought of as your "million dollar idea." But it's not only that. IP going OUT your door is, in fact, any intellectual property you are selling or giving away.

It also includes any intellectual property you are afraid that other people might steal from you.

The important thing to remember is that the stuff going OUT your door may be based on other people's stuff that came IN your door, not just the stuff you created from scratch.

Intellectual property is not only about you protecting your stuff from others; it's also about making sure that others can't use their intellectual property against you.

If somebody else's IP comes IN your door, by definition, it is going OUT of their door.

Just because you've managed to survive the early stages of your coaching business with no attacks, doesn't necessarily mean that this will continue to be the case as your business grows. If you are using someone's IP without permission and nobody is after you, this may mean several things:

 - you're too small for them to notice what you're doing;

- you're too small for them to care about what you're doing;

- they don't think that you have enough money for them to bother;

- they genuinely don't care about their IP going OUT their door; or

- they are genuinely happy that you are using their IP.

Unless you know for sure that they are happy with you using their IP (in which case, get them to confirm it in writing), you want to make sure that you have the right to use their IP to build anything that is critically important for your business.

Yes, few people are interested in suing a coach who is barely scraping by. However, as soon as you start seeing signs of success, people will suddenly remember all the tiny bits and pieces of their IP that you might have used while you were building your empire.

Do you want to become a source of passive income for people looking to make a quick buck?

Once lawyers recognize that you have deep pockets, they will be more than willing to bring a case against you on a contingency basis. *On a contingency basis* simply means the lawyer gets a percentage of whatever comes out of your pocket. Their clients love it for a very simple reason. They don't have to worry about paying the lawyer—the lawyer gets paid from the money *you* are going to shell out.

Lawyers only take cases on a contingency basis when they think there is a high likelihood they can get enough money for their clients that would more than cover the value of their time. In practical terms, this means that if you have a lot of money and happened to have violated someone's IP, lawyers will be lining up around the block to sue you into oblivion.

So, even if you don't care about protecting your own intellectual property, you still need to be concerned about the intellectual property of others that you may bring IN your door—to ensure that you protect your pockets.

WHAT'S AHEAD?

The rest of this book will address several intellectual property issues that are specifically relevant to coaches, mentors, trainers, and consultants.

Chapter 1 will deal with trademarks. Every successful coaching business treasures its brand. And the way to protect it is by registering it as a trademark.

Chapter 2 is about content. How do you make sure that all the stuff that you create and pay others to create for you is actually yours? In this chapter, you will learn how copyright works and how to address things the vast majority of business owners are not aware of. You will also learn how to properly turn your content into info-products that will allow you to make passive income off your knowledge and experience.

Chapter 3 is mostly about trade secrets. In this chapter, you will learn how can you protect your programs, client lists, and other confidential information. I will also briefly touch on protecting substantial inventions through patents.

After summing everything up, at the end of this book, I will share my story. If you care to find out how I became an intellectual property lawyer and what made me passionate about what I do—that's the place to look for it.

Now that you know what's ahead, let's just jump right into it. Turn the page—and learn all you need to know about protecting your brand through trademarks!

PROTECTING YOUR BRAND THROUGH TRADEMARKS

ONE PARAGRAPH SUMMARY

If you value your brand, you need to protect it by registering it as a trademark. Start with requesting your free trademark search and opinion at *http://freeTMsearch.com* and order the *All-Inclusive* trademark registration package from the Trademark Factory® at *http://trademarkfactory.com*.

You should never forget what business you're in. You're not in the business of dispensing advice and information. You are in the business of encouraging and helping people get better at what they do. You are in the business of leading by example.

Leading by example is all about branding. And if your business is about branding, then it's only reasonable that you should protect your brand.

That's what trademarks are for.

There are three eternal truths about trademarks.

1| Every successful business protects them. You will not find a single truly successful business (inside or outside of the coaching industry) that doesn't care about its brand. They've done at least something (some did more, some did less, but they've *all* done something) to protect their brand.

2| Trademarks are like fire insurance. You never want to actually *need* to have a trademark. The reason I'm comparing trademarks with fire insurance is because you don't get upset if you have fire insurance and your house does *not* burn down. In the same way, you don't get upset if you have a registered trademark and you never have a chance to sue someone who stole your brand. That's not what trademarks are for. They are to prevent infringements from happening.

3| You wouldn't let your child go to a battlefield without protective gear and ammo. You know better than anyone that the coaching industry is a very competitive battlefield, and your business with its brand is your baby. Trademarks are designed to give your baby a chance to survive in a competitive environment.

Before we move on, you must understand what trademarks are. The reason I say this is that most coaches are confused by it.

A trademark is a feature unrelated to the characteristics of your products or services which allows your business to help customers and consumers distinguish your products and services from identical or similar products and services of everyone else.

Let me rephrase it: A trademark can be *anything* (a name, a logo, a tagline, a sound, a color, a shape, or the look and feel of a product) as long as it has nothing to do with the functionality or features of your products and services and as long as it allows your customers to tell your products and services from the same or similar products and services offered by your competition.

> **Trademarks protect that which sets your product or service apart from all other similar products and services.**

Trademarks are not designed to protect the products or services themselves. They protect that which identifies *your* product or service and sets it apart from all other similar products and services.

Oh, and if you are the only business on the market that offers your particular product or service, you need to *imagine* that you have competitors who offer exactly the same products or services that you offer. Will your brand *still* allow your guests to distinguish your stuff from your competitors' stuff?

The best thing about trademarks is that they are the only type of intellectual property that can be protected forever. Unregistered trademarks are protected for as long as the business carries on and continues to use them. For registered trademarks, you will need to renew the registration. In most countries, you have to renew your trademark registrations every ten years. In Canada, you currently have to renew your trademark registration every fifteen years but this will soon change to ten years as Canada harmonizes its trademark laws with the rest of the world.

This book is not a comprehensive textbook on trademarks. It only contains information directly relevant to coaches and consultants.

For a more detailed (yet still in plain English) overview of trademark law, download my ebook *The Ultimate Insider's Guide to Trademarks*, a chapter from my best-selling book, *The Ultimate Insider's Guide to Intellectual Property* as part of your bonus package at *http://FacelessToLegendary.com/bonus*

MAIN TYPES OF TRADEMARKS

There are six main things coaches usually trademark:

- *Name of the company.* If your coaching business is more than just you coaching clients one-on-one, you probably came up with a name for your business as a whole. For example, T. Harv Eker didn't call his business Eker Consulting. He called it *Peak Potentials*®, which immediately showed his intention of building it as a scalable business, rather than as a job for himself.

– *Name of a program or a course.* If you teach more than one thing, you probably have different programs or courses. It is common to trademark such names. Think *The 4-Hour Workweek*®. Anybody can teach productivity, but only Tim Ferriss can call his programs 4-Hour Workweek.

– *Logos.* These are what you use to visually identify your company or your courses. For example, Tony Robbins trademarked his logo.

– *Taglines.* You use taglines to identify your company or courses. *The Path to Wellness Begins Here*® by Deepak Chopra is a good example.

– *Graphic representation of the system.* If you have a system of courses or if you came up with a graphic representation that conclusively explains one of your ideas, you can trademark the image. For example, Robert Kiyosaki trademarked his Cashflow Quadrant: . You will read more on this type of trademarks below.

WHY YOUR BRAND IS MORE IMPORTANT THAN YOUR DATA

There is a ton of content out there. One can spend a lifetime reading books and watching YouTube videos on whatever topic you specialize in. Even if some of these books and videos were authored by *you*—and if you are seriously planning to become legendary, you *got to have* books and videos authored by you,—your content is not what's going to make your prospects, in the words of Dan Kennedy, choose you vs. any and every other competitive option available to them, including doing nothing.

Your success as a coach depends on your ability to create the perception that not only you *know* your stuff better than your competition but that you have some sort of a *secret weapon* that helps people get from where they are to where they want to be.

You don't win clients by overwhelming people with a data dump, no matter how valuable your information might be. You win clients by showing them that you have a *system* that will allow people who are not as knowledgeable and experienced as you are to quickly and reliably learn from you and act on what they've learned.

Nobody cares about the brilliance of your internal systems until you have externalized them by making these systems a part of your packaging and branding.

At the very least, your system must have a memorable name. For your prospects and customers, if you don't have a name for your system, you don't *have* a system.

If you have a whole array of programs or courses, you can take it one step further and come up with a graphic representation of these programs. A great example comes from Colin Sprake's Make Your Mark. In addition to offering their courses à la carte, they offer them in packages:

Visualizations like these are perfect candidates for trademarking, because they are what your customers end up remembering your systems for.

And this is more than just about remembering. Visualizations like that imply that whoever came up with them knows what they're doing. It telegraphs that they are not simply trying to sell you as many courses as possible. They actually have a system where going through all of these courses in a specific order makes sense. From the sales and marketing perspective, this is a lot more convincing than simply telling students that they can pick any of 15 available programs.

This brings me to a very clever trick that successful businesses use to build and maintain a competitive advantage by creating an impression of uniqueness.

A while ago Ford was running commercials that ended with "Only Ford has Ecoboost fuel economy." Interestingly enough, nowhere in the ad did they tell you what Ecoboost fuel economy actually was. They didn't waste time telling you how it's better or even different from the competition. The only thing they told you was that Ford was the only company that had it. To make such a claim, Ford didn't need to invest millions in research and development. All they had to do was trademark the name!

Another example, Starbucks came across a drink. They knew they couldn't protect the recipe. They knew they wouldn't be able to stop competitors from offering the same type of drink. What did Starbucks do? They gave the drink a name, Frappuccino, and they trademarked it. Now they can legitimately claim that they are the only coffee place in the world where you can get your Frappuccino. (To be completely accurate, it was *The Coffee Connection* that came up with the name and Starbucks simply bought them out. If anything, this only shows how important protecting intellectual property can be, because it played a major role in Starbucks's decision to acquire *The Coffee Connection*.)

FedEx came up with an idea that people would appreciate if they could send their stuff knowing that it's going to reach the addressee quickly and reliably. FedEx also knew that at some point, whatever systems they came up with to offer their guaranteed deliveries would be replicated by the competition. So they came up with their famous tagline, *When it absolutely, positively has to be there overnight.* Owning that tagline was not enough to stop the competition from offering overnight deliveries, but it was more than enough to grow FedEx into a massive player in the delivery industry.

Likewise, trademarking the Cashflow Quadrant did not give Robert Kiyosaki a way to protect the underlying idea of four types of income, but it allowed him to legally prevent others from copying its visual representation. In many cases, for all practical intents and purposes, this is all you need to protect the idea or the system itself.

No matter how good your data, it's not the reason why people choose your services, it's not the reason you will become successful. As Blair Singer teaches, "Context is more important than content." Successful coaches have long realized that how they package their content and how they brand themselves and their business is what determines their success.

Trademarks is how you protect such context. Having said that, a trademark doesn't give you a monopoly over the word, slogan, or image you chose as your brand. You only have a monopoly over the *association* between that word, slogan, or image and the specific products or services that you offer.

> **Trademarks only give you a monopoly over the association between your brand and the specific products or services that you offer.**

For example, Jack Canfield does not own the phrase *"Chicken Soup"*—except for the products (books and audiobooks) and services (educational services) that he has registered his trademarks for. Restaurants and instant noodle makers can legally use the same phrase because they are not associated with books or education.

THREE MAIN REASONS TO TRADEMARK YOUR BRANDS

Simply put, *If It's Worth Promoting, It's Worth Protecting!*™. And yes, this tagline is our trademark.

> **If It's Worth Promoting, It's Worth Protecting!™**

There are three main reasons to trademark your brands.

1| A registered trademark is a very inexpensive way to ***minimize the risk of customer confusion.***

There are two types of customer confusion that a trademark registration can prevent.

The first is when your potential customers end up being coached by your competitor thinking that they are being coached by someone from *your* company. Imagine someone who has a vague recollection of your brand, but who doesn't really know how many trainers work under your brand. They do a quick Google search, see a familiar name, check out a website, look through the benefits you offer, they schedule their first session, and they arrive. Only they arrive to be greeted by someone else. All your marketing and advertising dollars just put money in someone else's pockets.

The second scenario is even worse. Imagine a customer who had a horrible experience with a trainer who uses the same name as yours. It could even be a trainer in a different city or province. The trainer was hungover, he kept picking up the phone to talk to other clients, the coffee was cold, and no refund was offered. Expect a Yelp review about *your* coaching company. Your future potential clients will find the review on Google—and find a diffferent trainer.

> **Imagine a customer who had a horrible experience with a trainer who uses the same name as yours leaving a Yelp review about *your* coaching company.**

There is a reason you created your branding and invested in marketing it. Don't lose your customers by letting your direct and indirect competitors take advantage of your brand or worse yet, ruin it.

21 A registered trademark is the best *insurance policy against forced rebranding.*

Let's take it one step further. What if another coach in a different city uses the same name as you, and they register it as their trademark?

Trademark registration protects your brand federally. A Canadian trademark protects your brand everywhere in Canada. A U.S. trademark protects your brand everywhere in the United States.

This means that if an Edmonton coach trademarks his name, nobody can use the same or a similar name in Montreal, Toronto, or Vancouver—even if no one there has ever heard about that Edmonton coach.

Imagine a situation when you've been running your coaching business in Vancouver for several years and one day you get a nasty letter from a lawyer, saying something like:

"Dear Coach,

I act for ABC Coaching in Edmonton that has a registered trademark for ABC.

It has come to my attention that you have been using the name ABC which is identical to my client's trademark.

This constitutes trademark infringement.

In order to avoid legal proceedings, my client demands that you:

- *change the name of your coaching company to a name that does not include ABC forthwith but no later than ten business days after the date of this letter;*

- *account for all proceeds collected by you and your company during the last twenty-four months; and*

- *within twenty days, pay my client 25 percent of the proceeds collected by you and your company during the last twenty-four months.*

Should you fail or neglect to satisfy my client's demands set out above, I have instructions to commence legal proceedings against you and will seek an injunction that will prevent your coaching company from unlawfully using my client's trademark.

Best regards,

Nasty Lawyer from a big law firm."

At that point, you would only have two options.

You could get involved in a long legal battle. And trust me, you don't want to be in this situation *even if you're right.* Why? The Edmonton coaching company has a trademark registration, so now it's up to you to prove to the judge that their trademark should never have been registered and that you have a prior right. Remember, legal battles are not cheap—especially if you have to do all the proving. We are talking dozens or even hundreds of thousands of dollars. On top of that, dealing with litigators and judges will take away the focus you need to build a successful coaching business.

> **Imagine receiving a letter from a lawyer demanding that you immediately rebrand.**

The second option would be to rebrand. Change all your signage, letterheads, flyers, business cards, websites, advertising—everything. This one isn't cheap either.

If you have a registered trademark, all you need to do is show the registration certificate to the judge. Now, it's up to the other side to challenge its validity. Litigation often becomes a matter of which side has more money to burn until the other side comes to their senses and gives up. You always want the other side having to prove something.

Just to be clear. Registering a trademark will not eliminate this risk completely, but it will minimize the risk of this happening at a cost that is barely noticeable.

3| A registered trademark has *intrinsic value*.

No matter what your opinion is on the teaching style of T. Harv Eker or the educational value of his courses, you'd be crazy not to want to own 100 percent of the business he created, Peak Potentials (recently rebranded as *New Peaks*). Why? Because it's a brand that is worth millions.

This brand is worth an extraordinary amount of money not because it offers great content, but because it's a brand that identifies a very successful business that a lot of people want to become a part of.

If your coaching business grows and you want to sell licenses or franchises, having your brand trademarked is a must. A well-protected, recognizable brand is the reason someone may want to work under your name, as opposed to starting their own from scratch. Licensing of intellectual property is one of the major streams of passive income and is how T. Harv Eker made a fortune on his programs.

> **If your coaching business grows and you want to sell licenses or franchises, having your brand trademarked is a must.**

You say, you won't ever become the next T. Harv Eker? OK. How about the next Tim Ferriss? It may seem like he's been around forever, but his 4-hour empire only started in 2007. Among many others, his company now owns multiple 4-hour trademarks ("THE 4-HOUR COOK", "THE 4-HOUR CHEF", "THE 4-HOUR BODY", "THE 4-HOUR", "THE 4-HOUR WORKWEEK"). The 4-hour brand is what allows him to generate interest to his teachings.

Similarly, Michael Gerber has been using his "E-Myth" brand to co-author The E-Myth Real Estate Invesor, The E-Myth Veterinarian, The E-Myth Bookkeeper, The E-Myth Nutritionist, The E-Myth Dentist, The E-Myth Insurance Store, The E-Myth Real Estate Brokerage, The E-Myth Architect, The E-Myth Financial Advisor, The E-Myth Landscape Contractor, The E-Myth Chiropractor, The E-Myth Optometrist, The E-Myth Attorney, The E-Myth Accountant, The

E-Myth Physician, and The E-Myth Contractor. The reason all of his co-authors were lining up to publish a book about how successful they were in using systems in their profession was that they wanted to be associated with Michael Gerber and his famous brand.

Even if you are not planning to franchise out or expand, at some point, a successful coaching business will transcend its owners. If you were to sell the business or leave it to your heirs, all goodwill in the brand must be passed along as well, which is precisely what trademarks are all about.

UNREGISTERED (COMMON-LAW) TRADEMARKS

In most countries, unregistered trademarks are not protected. In other words, no registration—no protection.

Unlike the rest of the world, Canada and the United States afford some limited protection to trademarks that have not been registered. A brand owner can recover damages it incurred as a result of a competitor selling products or services while passing them off to be the products or services of the brand owner. In legal speak, it is called the *tort of passing-off*.

However, such protection depends on how actively you use your trademarks in association with your products and services. This means that in order to stop competitors from using your unregistered trademark, not only do you have to prove that your mark is distinctive, you also have to prove, through surveys, that your trademark is well known to the public in the specific area where it is being used by your competitors.

In other words, if people know the unregistered brand of your coaching business in Toronto and Los Angeles, then you have a chance of preventing your competitors from running workshops under the same branding in Ontario and California. But there is nothing you can do with competitors who may wish to offer workshops under *your* brand in Calgary or New York.

This is different from a registered trademark where your certificate of registration is sufficient to protect you all across the country where the trademark is registered, and you don't have to prove how well people know your trademark.

If there is one thing that is really expensive in court, it is having to prove something. With all the required expert reports, surveys, affidavits, witnesses, and additional lawyering, every important issue you need to prove to the judge can easily be a matter of an extra $30,000–$50,000, if not more.

> **Having to prove something in court is really expensive. With a registered trademark, you don't have to prove that you own your brand.**

Once you realize that your trademarks may have current or future value, you should register them. While you may be flattered by others imitating your brand, the last thing you want is to spend tens of thousands of dollars and years of your life fighting over something that could have been easily protected when you were just starting out.

TRADEMARKS VS. TRADE NAMES

Company names (also known as trade names or business names)

are not the same as trademarks.

Simply incorporating the business or registering a DBA (*doing business as...*) name is not enough. All it does is prevent your competitors from registering an identical or similar name as their *corporate* name. However, such registration does nothing outside the province or the state where your coaching business is incorporated. It also does very little to protect you against competitors who might use your brand without using it as part of their corporate name or their DBA name.

Just as in the case of unregistered trademarks, prior use of a trade name *can* help you ultimately succeed in a dispute over your brand. However, a registered trademark will save you a lot of time and tens of thousands of dollars in legal fees.

Simply incorporating the business is not enough.

For example, if you incorporate your company as Quick Bucks Financial Training Ltd. in British Columbia, it doesn't mean that you now have a trademark for *Quick Bucks* or *Quick Bucks Financial Training*.

It doesn't become your trademark until you start using it *as a trademark*. And even then, unless you are famous all across Canada, anyone can *legally* start their own Quick Bucks training company in Alberta or Ontario.

Only registered trademarks allow you to protect your brand throughout the country.

SEVEN BENEFITS OF TRADEMARK REGISTRATION

While unregistered trademarks are afforded some limited protection in Canada and the United States, there are significant benefits that come with registration.

> **There are significant benefits that come with registering trademarks.**

PROTECTION IS FEDERAL

Registration grants you the exclusive right to use your trademark all across Canada or the States, whereas unregistered trademarks can only protect you in geographical areas where you can prove that your brand is known to enough customers. With a registered trademark, you don't need to worry about whether you've established sufficient goodwill in a particular area. A registered trademark protects you in the most remote locations of Canada and the United States where nobody has even heard of your brand.

Just to be clear, trademarks are registered on a per-country basis, so your Canadian trademark registration protects you in Canada, and your U.S. trademark registration protects you in the United States. But your Canadian trademark registration does not automatically protect you in the United States and your U.S. registration does not automatically protect you in Canada or other countries.

PROTECTION BEFORE USE

In Canada and the States, your unregistered trademarks are only protected in the geographical area where people know that you exist. People can only know that you exist *after* you have started using your brand. So you have to have been using the brand for quite some time to be able to prove to the judge that you have a reputation worthy of protection.

When you apply for a trademark, nobody needs to know that you exist. You may not have even started using the brand, but you are already protected. This is called registration on the "proposed use" basis in Canada and registration on the "intent to use" basis in the States. Once you have filed the application, the Trademarks Office will not allow anyone else to register a subsequent identical or a confusingly similar trademark. If you know that your new brand will generate some buzz, apply to register it as a trademark before you share it with the world.

PRESUMPTION OF VALIDITY AND OWNERSHIP

If you have an unregistered trademark and you find yourself in the middle of a lawsuit over your brand, you will need to prove to the judge that your brand is a trademark, that you have been using it as a trademark, that enough people know you have been using it as a trademark, and that the infringer knew you have been using it as a trademark. It's tough. You need witnesses, expert reports, surveys, and legal arguments. All of this costs a ton of money.

A certificate of trademark registration is evidence that your brand is a valid trademark and that you own it. Showing the certificate to the judge is sufficient to establish rights to the trademark. Now it's up to the other side to prove that you don't own it.

If I'm repeating myself (and I am), it's only because this is crucially important. Having to prove something to the judge is really expensive.

A VALUABLE ASSET

I already explained why a brand has intrinsic value for every successful business. Now think about this, if your brand is valuable, wouldn't a piece of paper that ensures that no one can use your brand without your permission also be tremendously valuable? Registered trademarks allow you to maintain your competitive advantage through a government-backed monopoly, and because of that they are regarded as one of the most valuable assets of every successful coaching business.

THE GOVERNMENT IS WORKING—
SO YOU DON'T HAVE TO

A registered trademark gives you free and automatic protection. Here's what I mean. Every trademark application is reviewed by a trademarks examiner in the Trademarks Office (the Canadian Intellectual Property Office in Canada or the U.S. Patent and Trademarks Office in the United States). The first thing the trademarks examiner does when a trademark application hits their desk is conduct a trademark search to make sure that no one has already registered or applied for a confusingly similar trademark. And if somebody has, then they are going to reject the later trademark application citing the prior one.

The beauty of this is that the owner of the prior trademark does not need to do anything. They may not even know about the subsequent trademark application. The government is doing everything for them.

NOW PEOPLE KNOW IT

People who are experienced in branding know that their brilliant ideas may have already visited someone else. So they always check the public database of registered trademarks to make sure that no one has registered a trademark similar to the brand they came up with, and that they can safely adopt, use and protect that brand.

If they see that the name is already "taken", they will likely pivot at that early stage and come up with a different name.

Because the database of registered trademarks is open to the public in both Canada and the United States, the information that it contains about your trademark serves as public notice that you have a claim to exclusivity to your brand. This means that everyone else is deemed to have known that you have a registered trademark and unauthorized use of the brand will be deemed to constitute deliberate infringement.

WORLDWIDE PROTECTION

Registering your brand as a trademark in your home country makes it much simpler to protect your brand worldwide.

For example, while you can apply for a trademark before you start using it in Canada, the registration will not be issued until you have started using it. The brand is still protected, it's just not registered yet. However, if you have registered your brand in your home country and are interested in protecting it in another country *before* you start using it there, all you need to do is let the trademark examiner know that you are relying on your foreign registration.

CAN YOU REGISTER YOUR TRADEMARKS?

This is really the first thing to figure out. If your brand is not trade-markable, that's often the end of the conversation. So how do you know if you can register your trademarks?

I like to say that *if it's remarkable, it's trademarkable*®. But things are slightly more complicated than that.

> **If It's Remarkable, It's Trademarkable!®**

You need to avoid two big traps before you can confirm that you CAN register your trademark—they are called the *absolute* and the *relative* grounds for refusal. If your trademark is not refused on either of these grounds, it CAN be registered.

ABSOLUTE GROUNDS

Because the function of a trademark is to distinguish your products and services from similar or identical products and services of others and is not meant to give you a monopoly over those products and services themselves, there are a number of things that cannot function as trademarks or that cannot be registered as trademarks.

You are not allowed to claim the **generic name** of a product or a service as your trademark. For example, you can't trademark COACH-ING or WORKSHOPS to prevent your competitors from using these words in the names of their programs. Remember, the function of a trademark is to distinguish your coaching business from all others, not to give you the right to say, "*I am the only company that can offer* *coaching services in Canada.*"

> **You are not allowed to claim the generic name of a product or a service as your trademark.**

Some legitimate trademarks have become generic through their wide use. This happens when you miss the moment when your products and services are no longer one of the kind, they become *the* kind. Trademarks that become generic names can no longer function as trademarks and therefore nobody can claim a monopoly over them anymore, whether through registration or otherwise.

Next to generic names are **clearly descriptive or deceptively misdescriptive** marks.

In plain English, *clearly descriptive* means that your trademark is made up of dictionary words (or their phonetic equivalents) which describe some important characteristics of your product or service. For example, you can't trademark DOWNTOWN TORONTO PERSONAL TRAINING or B1Z KoacH.

Deceptively misdescriptive means that your trademark is made up of dictionary words (or their phonetic equivalents) that would mislead consumers into believing that your products or services have characteristics that they do not possess. For example, you can't trademark MASTER NLP IN 60 MINUTES if your program does not result in mastery of NLP in an hour. Likewise, you can't trademark TRILLIONAIRE MASTERMIND GROUP if your group does not do masterminding or if it does not have trillionaire members in it.

You cannot register clearly descriptive or deceptively misdescriptive marks unless you have used them to such an extent that everyone has come to associate your business with that particular name. Until that happens (and it typically takes several years), you can still use such marks in the hope that you will acquire the reputation required to render them registrable. For example, if you have been using TRILLIONAIRE MASTERMIND GROUP for so long that a substantial number of people across the country understand that they will be buying from *you* rather than simply think that they would be buying a membership in a group where they can pick a trillionaire's brain, then your deceptively misdescriptive trademark may become registrable. This is not an easy task though.

In Canada, while you can *use* your **personal name** as a trademark, as a general rule, you can't *register* a trademark that consists only of your full name or your last name. For example, JOHN SMITH or SMITH would not be registrable.

There are a few exceptions to the rule, however.

If your trademark consists of more than just your name, it will become registrable. For example, JOHN SMITH'S COACHING no longer violates the rule.

Also, just as in the case of descriptive marks, if you have such a reputation that everyone associates your name with your services, then the name can be registered as a trademark. However, you need to be really well known for this to work. Think Napolen Hill or Brian Tracy kind of fame.

Simply using the first name (but not the last name) as a trademark does not violate the rule. So JOHN, JOHN'S, AT JOHN'S and JOHN'S TRAINING would all be registrable trademarks.

Combining several names into one trademark is another way out, for example, SMITH & WESSON would be registrable.

Finally, you cannot trademark something that goes to the **functionality** of the product itself. Anything that is required in order for the product to function cannot be protected as a trademark. If anything, it should be protected through a patent.

One of the prominent features of accelerated learning method of teaching is constantly asking audience questions and demanding a response. T. Harv Eker and other New Peaks' trainers are famous for always saying, "Yes or yes?", "Good or good?", "True or true?", "Turn to someone and give them a high five", etc. All of these questions and phrases may be very effective during training but cannot be trademarked in order to stop other trainers from using them in their workshops. In other words, even if you are successful in trademarking "YES OR YES" for seminars in the field of personal development", you would only be able to stop your competitors from *calling* their companies or their courses "YES OR YES", but you would not be able to use your trademark to stop other trainers from interjecting their content with "Yes or yes" questions.

Tony Robbins was able to trademark the phrase "FEAR INTO POWER—THE FIREWALK EXPERIENCE", but while the trademark was well suited to prevent others from using the phrase as a tagline, it could not be used to stop others from setting up their versions of his walk-on-hot-coals challenge.

So during the absolute grounds review, the Trademarks Office will confirm that your trademark fulfills its proper purpose of distinguishing your products and services from identical or similar products or services of other companies and that it does not fall under any of the categories that the law says cannot be trademarked. When your trademark has passed this hurdle, you can move on to the next step.

RELATIVE GROUNDS

The next step is to ensure that your trademark is not identical or confusingly similar with another previously registered or applied for trademark.

> **Ensure that your trademark is not identical or confusingly similar with another previously registered or applied for trademark.**

FIND OUT IF YOUR BRAND IS TRADEMARKABLE

The problem is, most business owners don't have a clue how to conduct these searches and how to properly interpret the results they're getting. A trademark search is much more involved than simply typing in your brand name into the *trademark* field and clicking the *Search Now* button.

Most firms charge $200-$300 for their professionals to conduct a trademark search for you and write an opinion that explains whether your trademark can be registered and why.

On the other hand, online filing websites will lure you with their automated trademark searches that are extremely unreliable, if not outright dangerous. For example, *Trademarkia* will readily offer you to apply for "MICRO-SOFT SOFTWARE" trademark because no identical trademark exists in the database. Guess how long it will be before you hear from Microsoft's lawyers if you rely on such search!

I pride myself on launching the Trademark Factory®, the most streamlined full-scope trademarking service in the world. And as part of our services, we offer to conduct your trademark search and prepare the registrability opinion *for free.*

Let me say it again. You're getting real people, trademark agents and attorneys, to manually search the databases for you, analyze the results, and walk you through the registrability report over the phone for free, risk-free, with no strings attached. Is this a great deal or what?

If you have a brand that you think is worth trademarking, just fill out the form at ***http://freeTMsearch.com*** – and we'll take it from there. We will get back to you within two business days, and actually go over the registrability report with you to make sure you understand where your brand is at. This way, you are not just getting a list of identical and similar trademarks, you are getting clarity as to whether your trademarks can be registered.

Even if you are just THINKING about a new brand, don't worry. This is completely confidential. I guarantee that we will never use or disclose your information against your interests. Trust me, you will be in good hands with us.

Just to be clear, if your brand is trademarkable, we *will* offer our services to get it trademarked. We will show you the packages that we offer and demonstrate that we have the best offer on the market. But you are under no obligation to buy anything from us.

So again, go to ***http://freeTMsearch.com*** right now and order your free trademark search from us.

In Canada and the United States, the databases of registered trademarks are public information, and anyone can do a search to check if there are other brands similar to yours that have been previously registered or applied for.

To wrap this up, if your trademark is not unregistrable under the absolute grounds for refusal and is not confusingly similar with other previously registered or applied for trademarks, then it CAN be registered.

The next thing to decide is whether you SHOULD register your trademark.

SHOULD YOU REGISTER YOUR TRADEMARKS?

Once you have established that you have something that meets the requirements for a trademark, you have to take it one step further and figure out if you SHOULD register it. Just because you CAN register your trademarks doesn't mean that you always SHOULD.

Wouldn't it be nice if you could ask yourself three simple questions and know exactly whether you should be spending money on trademarking your brand?

Well, guess what! I came up with three questions that are going to do exactly that.

Sit down, relax, close your eyes and imagine that you have achieved everything you've been dreaming of for your business. This is very personal to you. Only you know what you are trying to build. It can be becoming the best coach in town, or it can be building the most influential training company on the planet. One thing I know for sure, if you're reading this book, it won't be about squeezing just enough people into buying your programs so that you wouldn't have to look for a "real job".

So again, visualize your coaching business at its height. It's at its peak. Everything happened just the way you hoped.

Now imagine opening a letter from a lawyer representing some other trainer.

The letter demands that you abandon your branding and change it to something completely different.

Then ask yourself the first question. Would it be a problem if someone tried to force you to rebrand your courses?

> **Would it be a problem if someone tried to force you to rebrand?**

Can you quietly walk away from the brand without losing a lot of money? Will you?

If the cost of rebranding would be high or if you think you might consider fighting over this in court— register your trademarks.

As you will learn in this book, you can trademark your brand for less than what one extra client is worth to you. And the registration can last forever. Trust me, you will always be busy with other things. Don't put off the decision to trademark your brand until it's too late.

OK. Let's say the dreadful letter never comes. Instead, your coaching business is flourishing, just like you hoped it would.

Then you notice another trainer advertizing his programs using *your* brand.

How does that make you feel?

> **What if your competitor uses your name or tagline to advertise *their* coaching programs?**

If you think you might consider fighting over this in court—register your trademarks. Your lawyer may not be happy because when you have registered your trademarks, the lawyer will spend a lot less time arguing your case (so you end up paying much less in legal fees). But you're in the business to make your clients happy and make a healthy profit—not to make your lawyers happy.

Finally, ask yourself, **what's the next step?**

Will your brand help you get more money for your coaching business if you decide to franchise, license out, expand or sell it in the future?

If your plans involve franchising, licensing out, expanding or selling your business, it should be clear as day that you should trademark your brand. The only reason someone may want to become your franchisee is because you have developed a brand that will get enough people into their seats to justify the franchising fee. Your brand is what your franchisees and licensees are buying so it only makes sense to protect it.

> **Will there be any value in your brand as you franchise, license out, expand or sell your coaching business in the future?**

But even if you are a solo coach with no plans of expansion, do you plan to live forever? If you think that whoever takes over your coaching business would benefit from keeping the brand, do them (and yourself) a favour and protect the goodwill associated with your brand.

> In fact, *"we're too small / it's too early"* is the number one myth about trademark registration. We hear it all the time, but it does not make this statement any more correct.
>
> You are running a coaching business. It's not a hobby. It's a business.
>
> It is crucial that you get it right.
>
> Read about this myth as well as seven others in our *8 Most Dangerous Myths about Trademark Registration* report that you can download as part of your bonus package at *http:// FacelessToLegendary.com/bonus*

This three-question test is not some sort of trickery designed to compel you to register your trademarks regardless of where you are with your business. If it sounds like a very simplistic way to make a decision, it's because it *is*!

The only legitimate reason *not* to trademark your brand is when— even in the best-case scenario for your coaching business—your brand would still have no value and you could walk away from it with no regrets or losses.

Which should actually lead you to think, *why am I investing in a brand with no value?*

Otherwise, protect your brand as early as you can. You should trademark your brand *as soon as you realize that you would fight not to lose it.* Remember, trademarks are just like fire insurance. You can't buy one when your house is already on fire. Protect your brand before you need to fight with someone over it.

Again, *if it's worth promoting, it's worth protecting!*™

HOW DO YOU REGISTER YOUR TRADEMARKS?

Once you know that you CAN and that you SHOULD register your trademarks, the final step is to figure out HOW to do it.

I created the *Trademark Factory*® to make this the easiest question for you to answer.

There used to be only three options for business owners when it came to trademarking.

You could *file your trademarks yourself.* This is an option for those who want to be their own accountants, mechanics and dentists. Aside from the issue that it's really easy to mess it up and do it wrong, is it really the best use of your time to file your own trademarks?

> **Is it really the best use of your time to file your own trademarks?**

When you are not represented by a trademark professional, you are much more likely to receive a letter from the Trademarks Office. The letter is called an office action (or an "examiner's report") and its purpose is to inform you that your trademark application does not meet their standards. Many unrepresented applicants have no idea how to respond to these office actions, and abandon their trademark applications at this stage.

We often get requests from business owners who filed their own applications and now need them fixed. Their strategy was to see if the application would go through without the expense of hiring a professional. The problem with this approach is that often self-represented applicants draft their applications so poorly that there is nothing we or anybody else can do to fix them.

Another option was to **use online trademark filing websites**. They have automated the filing process to make it easier for business owners to figure out what should go where. They will file your applications for $199, $299, or $399 based on what YOU are going to tell them. But guess what? If something goes wrong, and it happens in more than half of the cases, they are going to send you to one of the law firms that they are affiliated with, and those lawyers are going to charge you an arm and a leg to fix your application. No wonder they are happy to take your money to apply for MICRO-SOFT SOFTWARE!

The third option was to **use a typical law firm**. In most cases, they will do everything right. But you won't know your budget until the whole process is over, and it usually takes fourteen to eighteen months. They'll send you their two-page schedule of fees, detailing that if *this* happens then they will be charging you *this* amount, and if *that* happens then they will be charging you *that* amount.

Thing is, few business owners know how the trademark registration process really works, so they naively assume that the amount they see next to "drafting and filing trademark application" covers the entire cost of registration as if the rest of the schedule of fees does not apply to them.

> **The problem with traditional law firms is not that they are expensive but that they are *unpredictably* expensive.**

Based on this assumption, they start comparing apples to oranges (filing fees with total fees) and end up buying a lemon. I've met dozens of business owners who were lured in by low filing fees, but ended up paying five, six and even seven thousand dollars for a single trademark. The problem is not that it's expensive. The problem is that it's UNPREDICTABLY expensive.

This problem is so pressing that we released the report *5 Trademarking Rip-Offs You Should Avoid.*

This report is part of the bonus package you can download at *http://FacelessToLegendary.com/bonus*

There HAD to be a better way. So I came up with the better way. It's called the **Trademark Factory®**.

We surveyed hundreds of entrepreneurs about the challenges they faced when dealing with traditional lawyers and trademark agents. We identified three big reasons why businesses are hesitant to use trademark professionals:

- There is no way to know how much it will end up costing you until you get the final of the many invoices for services;

- The application is filed by a clerk, and the lawyer does not see it until there is something wrong with it, at which point you start getting billed by the hour; and

- If something goes wrong, you don't get your money back because you are paying for a lawyer's time, not the results.

We built the *Trademark Factory*® to address all of these concerns and to make it as easy as possible for business owners to protect their valuable brands.

We are the first and the only firm on the planet that will offer you an ALL-INCLUSIVE package that will cover the cost of the entire process, from filing to registration for a single, all-inclusive flat fee. If it takes us three hours or three hundred hours to deal with the examiners at the Trademarks Office, your price stays the same. The only thing it does not include is opposition proceedings that third parties may initiate against your application *after* it has been approved by the Trademarks Office. But don't worry, opposition proceedings only happen in just a fraction of one percent of cases. And if you want even more protection that would also cover unexpected oppositions, you can choose our ULTIMATE package.

When we do a free trademark search for you, we will tell you about the registrability of your brand. In most cases, we will be able to offer you our unique 100% money-back guarantee. What this means is, if your trademark does not get approved, you get all of your money back. For many trademarks, we even offer a 100+% money-back guarantee, where you get back not only our fees, but also the government fees. So we refund more than we received from you.

Here's my philosophy: if we tell you that we think your trademark is registrable and take your money, and the government rejects it at the examination stage, it is *immoral* and *unethical* for us to keep your money, no matter how much time we spent on your file. It amazes me that we are the only law firm on the planet with this attitude!

We also guarantee that each and every file is reviewed by a registered trademark agent or a licensed trademark attorney. So it's not a clerk who does the work to be fixed by real professionals later. We do everything right the first time. Because we are not charging hourly rates with our ALL-INCLUSIVE package, our interests are naturally aligned with yours.

We call it the Triple-Peace-of-Mind Guarantee™.

HOW MUCH?

You may be wondering, how much does it cost to register a trademark.

As I explained above, the beauty of our All-Inclusive package is that I can answer this question with complete certainty and predictability—without having to publish a multi-page schedule of fees.

At the time of this publication, our All-Inclusive package is only CAD $1995 + tax + government fees.

A few comments are needed.

- This amount is per trademark per country;

- If you register more than one trademark in the same country, you will get a volume discount;

- If you are outside of Canada, there is no tax added to this amount, otherwise the tax will depend on your province (ranges from 5 to 13 percent);

- Government fees in Canada are calculated on a per-trademark basis and are CAD $450 per trademark (CAD $250 payable when you file the application and CAD $200 payable when the trademark is allowed);

- Government fees in the United States are calculated on a per-class basis and are USD $275 per class. All goods and services are divided into forty-five classes—thirty-four classes of products and eleven classes of services. Therefore, if you are filing your trademark in three classes (Class 41 - life coaching services; Class 16 - books; and Class 25 - T-Shirts), the government fees will be USD $825; and

- Even though the future price of our packages is subject to change without notice, we guarantee that when you order trademark registration services from us, you will know your entire budget to a penny before you spend a dime.

This buys you ten or fifteen years of trademark protection.

I can't think of many things of equal importance that you can buy for anything close to CAD $2000.

Just go over your budget for the previous year, and notice what you spent around CAD $2000 on. Car insurance? Cell phones? Cable and internet? Monthly rent? Two months' salary of your part-time assistant?

Trust me, protecting the brand of your coaching business is worth it.

TIPS & TRICKS

In addition to requesting your free trademark search and registrability opinion at *http://freeTMsearch.com* and using the Trademark Factory® to get your trademarks registered, there are a number of things you should do to protect your brand.

USE A TRADEMARK SYMBOL

Once you have decided to use a particular brand for your coaching business, start putting a trademark symbol (™) next to it.

What the ™ symbol says to the public is that you are using this logo, name, or tagline as your trademark. In fact, this means that you *yourself* think that it is your trademark. However, it has an added advantage because a lot of people don't know trademark laws and think that there is something more required from a business owner before they can place the ™ sign next to their brand. Customers may take you more seriously, even though all you had to do was insert an extra character in all of your branding and marketing materials.

Sometimes you'll see an "R" encircled (®). This means that the trademark is registered. While the ™ sign means that you yourself think that it is your trademark, the ® sign means that you think that it is your trademark, *and* the government agrees. Be careful, because you can get into a lot of trouble for using the ® symbol if your trademark is not actually registered. Don't use it if you only have an unregistered trademark. U.S. law carries some heavy penalties for unauthorized use of the ® symbol.

> **Use ™ next to unregistered trademarks and ® next to registered trademarks.**

Don't try to find the ™ sign on the keyboard. It's not there. But, if you are using Windows, you may hold down the ALT key followed by 0153 and you will see a nice TM sign (™) right there. In Microsoft Word, you can also hit CTRL + ALT + T to achieve the same result.

To get the registered trademark symbol, hold down the ALT key followed by 0174, or simply hit CTRL + ALT + R in Microsoft Word.

DOCUMENT YOUR USE OF YOUR BRAND

Keep logs of your use of the mark on your website. Make printouts. Save receipts from the printer shop where you printed your business cards. Save invoices of you selling your products bearing your trademarks. Try to save as much evidence of prior use as possible.

If there is a dispute about the priority to the trademark, the path to success would be to demonstrate prior use. Just because you told the Trademarks Office that you have been using the mark since 1890 is not enough. You must be able to back it up with evidence.

Make sure you have it.

REGISTER DOMAIN NAMES

You want to register your domain names before your brand becomes known because there will be a lot of people who will want to profit off your inability to foresee the value of your own brand. It's a lot easier (and cheaper) to buy a domain name at $8.99, compared to having to beg somebody to sell it to you for a few thousand dollars.

You may end up owning dozens of useless domain names at some point in time, but the investment is miniscule compared to what you may be saving if your brand becomes known and popular.

FromFaceless to Legendary for Coaches, Mentors, Trainers, and Consultants

For your convenience, we launched our own domain name registration website where you can buy your .COM domains for only USD $8.99. Check it out at *http://TMFDomains.com*.

NAMECHK.COM

NameChk.Com is an internet site which allows you to check over a hundred social media platforms to see if your name is available. Obviously, you won't need to register on all of these platforms, but there are several that can be very important for your business, such as Facebook, YouTube, Twitter, LinkedIn, Yelp, and possibly others.

If they're all taken, then it's an indication that you may run into problems with other people. If they are not taken, then you may want to go ahead and register them in your name so that when your brand becomes well known, you won't have to buy the names from somebody who was quicker to figure out the value of your brand.

YOU OWN YOUR CONTENT-INTENSIVE BUSINESS.
WHO OWNS YOUR CONTENT?

ONE PARAGRAPH SUMMARY

Make sure you have a proper paper trail for all of the content you use to run and promote your coaching business. A good starting point is the templates you can get at *http://NiceContracts.com*

SO WHO OWNS YOUR CONTENT?

From a strictly legal perspective, this chapter is about copyright. But I remember my promise not to turn this book into a law textbook. So for you, this chapter will be about content that you create and get others to create for you. I'm talking about your courses, books, websites, videos, illustrations, brochures, and other marketing materials.

This book is not a comprehensive textbook on copyright. It only contains information directly relevant to coaches and consultants.

For a more detailed (yet still in plain English) overview of copyright law, download my ebook *The Ultimate Insider's Guide to Copyright*, a chapter from my best-selling book, *The Ultimate Insider's Guide to Intellectual Property* as part of your bonus package at *http://FacelessToLegendary.com/bonus*

Copyright is a very powerful double-edged sword.

The good news is that as long as your content is minimally original and exists outside of your head so that others can perceive it in some shape or form, it's *automatically* protected by copyright. You don't have to register copyright in your books, videos, articles, or charts to claim protection. It's *already* there. Oh yeah, "original" does *not* mean brilliant, unique, unusual, unlike anything anyone has ever written, or one of a kind. "Original" in copyright terms simply means "*not copied from a pre-existing source.*"

This also happens to be the bad news, because the fact that you paid someone to have your website designed or your marketing copy written does not mean that you own copyright in that content—even if it was specifically created for you.

There is one important thing that you need to understand about how copyright works. Copyright only protects the way you express your ideas, not the underlying ideas themselves. So when you write a book, you will own copyright in the book, that is, in the sequence of words and sentences in it, but you will not own copyright in the general topic of the book. Just because Jack Canfield published a collection of inspirational stories in his famous *Chicken Soup for the Soul* series, does not mean that others can no longer publish inspirational stories. His copyright prevents people from copying the stories themselves, and his trademark prevents them from calling their books, *Chicken Soup for the Soul*, but beyond that, the underlying idea behind the book (or the series) is not protected.

> **Copyright does not protect ideas. Copyright protects original expression of ideas.**

The general rule is that whoever creates content owns copyright in it. When it's yourself, you should preserve evidence that it was you who created the content. When you're dealing with content created by someone else, you need to properly document the transfer of intellectual property in such content over to you.

And I mean "content" in the broadest possible sense. Think interface design, logos, images, illustrations, photos, fonts, HTML code, your videos, text on your website, ad copy, databases, web scripts, songs, jingles—the list goes on and on and on…

Most coaches hire, at one point or another, someone to design a website and to craft their marketing materials. Whether you use professional agencies and studios, crowdsourcing sites, college students, or your cousin's teenaged daughter, you and this creative person need to come to an agreement. You need to define each party's obligations with respect to the relationship as well as the responsibility for copyright clearances and clarity on copyright ownership.

> **Just because you paid someone to design your website or to write your marketing copy does not mean that you own copyright in that content.**

For the sake of simplicity, I will use the example of designers working on your website for the rest of this chapter. But all of the information is fully applicable to all other types of content.

According to most copyright laws, it is the person who actually created the design that is recognized as its author. Unless a true employment relationship exists between you and the designer and unless the creation of the website is within the scope of such employee's duties, the designer is also the first owner of copyright. This means that the only way for you to obtain copyright in the website is to enter into a written assignment or license agreement with the copyright owner (the designer).

I recently got a call from a really frustrated business owner. He told me that several years ago, he paid a web designer to build a website for him and a freelance photographer to take pictures of him for the website.

Now, he said, as his business evolved, he wanted to start using the photos in his offline printed marketing materials. He also made a few changes to the website to reflect the growth of his business.

"Can you imagine that?" he said. *"The photographer refused to give me the originals for free, and the web designers sent me a letter stating that I can't make changes on my own, and that I have to hire them, at some ridiculously high price!"*

I asked, *"Do you have a written contract with them?"*

He said, *"I don't have a contract with the photographer, but I do have a contract with the web designer."*

"What does your contract with the web designer say?" I asked. *"Well, it says that they will create this web design for me, and that I will pay them. So they created the web site, and I paid them. What else do I need?"*

"Does the contract say somewhere that they assign copyright in the web design and that you own it?" I asked.

He replied, *"No, but what does it matter if it says here, plain and simple, that they created it FOR ME?!"*

My response went along the lines of, *"This is the classic case of when you buy the tangible stuff without buying the IP behind it. All you got was a license to use it. Since you only have a license, not ownership, the company that built the website can contact you and demand that if you want any changes, you have to hire their company to implement them.*

"Even if you want to hire a new company, you can't—because you only have a license to use the website as is and you do not have the right to modify it. The company that built the website is the only one who has that right.

"They could also sell the same design to anyone else, including your competitor.

"And as for the photographer, she retained ownership in the photographs that she took of you as well. She can't sell them to others because of your personality rights, but you still don't own the copyright in them, because you never bought it from her."

After he shared with me what he would like to do to the photographer, the designer, lawyers, and those who write IP laws, he asked, *"So what are my options?"*

I said, *"There are three things you can do. One, you can just pay them what they are asking to make the necessary changes and get the necessary files. Two, you can renegotiate the agreement with them and do what you should have done in the first place, that is buy the IP outright, so that you don't have to have this conversation ever again. Three, you can redo the entire thing with someone else, making sure that the new website does not look anything like the old website and that you have a proper contract this time."*

Understandably, he hated all three options. But this is what you will be left with if you neglect to take proper care of the IP coming IN.

Here's the moral of the story. Simply because you paid for something doesn't necessarily mean that you own the intellectual property rights to it. A lot of people don't seem to realize this but often, what you are paying for is a *license* to use the IP, not actual *ownership* of the IP.

When you buy a book in the store, you own the paper on which it is printed, but you don't own the copyright in the story. When you download a program to your computer, you own the file, but you don't own the intellectual property in the software. When you buy a car with intermittent windshield wipers, you buy the car, including its intermittent windshield wipers, but you don't buy the patent that gives you the monopoly to build cars with intermittent windshield wipers. When you buy an iPhone, you buy the iPhone, but you don't buy Apple's logo or the iPhone trademark.

> **Have a written agreement assigning all intellectual property rights to you.**

I like to explain this using the analogy of buying a refrigerator. You want to make sure that you own both the fridge itself and the cold that it generates. One is kind of useless without the other. Granted, we don't run into these issues with refrigerators, but many business owners look at websites, marketing materials, software, and other content that they pay for exactly the same way. They assume that when they're buying the fridge, they're buying the cold as well. Not necessarily. When you are buying content from someone, make sure you buy both the embodiment (original images, prints, files, etc.) *and* the intellectual property to that content.

Just because you paid to have your website designed, does not mean that you own copyright in it.

A website to which you don't own copyright is not your asset, it is not something that you can offer an investor to buy a share of.

Unless the website has absolutely no value to you and you can quickly replace it without using any of the elements of the old design in your new design, always make sure that you have a written agreement with the web designer assigning all rights in the design to you.

This will also ensure that the designer will not have a legal right to "design" the same website for somebody else.

A judge may be sympathetic to your situation, given that you paid a lot of money for something, but if you don't have it in writing, there's really very little the judge can do. You still don't own the IP. At the very best, you will have a limited license to use it.

Here's what this usually means in plain terms:

- it's not your asset, so you can't sell it;

- it's still their asset, so they are free to sell it to whoever they want, including your competitors; and

- you can't make any changes to it without their permission.

This can be a big problem because when businesses hire people to create websites, marketing materials, videos, and similar content, they expect that they will own all rights to them and that their competitors will not have the legal right to have an identical website.

Whenever you have someone create content for you, make sure they sign an agreement stating that you own the product. If the person won't sign the contract, then look for someone who will. It's not enough to simply pay for something to be made for you—you need that contract as well.

Although oral contracts are good enough for most purposes, they are not good enough for the purpose of assignment of copyright. Canadian law is very specific in that the contract must be in writing. While the agreement does not necessarily have to be printed and signed, it is still the preferred way of documenting contractual relationships. If you have to enter into the agreement over email, make sure you can properly identify the other party to the transaction.

At ***http://NiceContracts.com***, I have made available several templates of intellectual property agreements. Most notably, you can download the template for an After-the-Fact Copyright Assignment agreement (which covers situations when you want to confirm that you own what had already been created for you) and a Content Creation Agreement (which covers situations when you are only *planning* to hire someone who will create something for you).

Oh yeah, one last thing, it's a lot easier to sign the right contact before your money has left your pocket and landed in the pocket of someone who has promised to do something for you. Most web designers would not have an issue signing a document that says you own the design they have created for you *before* they get paid to do the work. Getting them to sign something *after* they've already spent your money can be very difficult.

WHAT ABOUT YOUR EMPLOYEES?

One important exception to the rule that paying doesn't mean buying relates to employees.

If you have hired someone as an employee, then the law says that whatever they create within the scope of their employment duties belongs to you as the employer.

This only works if:

- there is a true employment relationship between you and the worker (i.e. the worker is a salaried employee);

- the IP was created within the scope of employment duties of the employee; and

- there is nothing in the employment agreement that says otherwise.

But it is really a poor practice to rely on the default provisions of various laws when you can back your arrangement up with a written contract that would also deal with important details that are not addressed in such laws. Remember, contracts are much clearer than laws. Or at least they should be.

> **Getting employees to sign a contract makes your life easier.**

The main reason for getting employees to sign a contract is that it just makes your life easier. You don't have to worry about arguing with an employee over ownership because it's already been settled before work has even begun. You don't have to argue whether creating certain types of IP is within the scope of the employee's duties because you would address that in the contract. You don't have to argue over whether the employee is to be paid extra if you use the IP. You don't have to argue over whether you should let the world know that the IP had been created by the employee. You don't have to consider whether the employee's dignity will suffer if you use the content they created for you in a modified form or in support of products or ideas that your employee may disagree with.

You don't have to argue over anything that you have properly addressed in a written agreement. That's what written agreements are for!

I guarantee that if you have written agreements with your employees where you properly address intellectual property issues, you'll thank me if your employee creates something for your business that generates you a lot of money, and you can point out to the overly eager employee that no, you own it, and no, they can't get a slice of your pie.

HOW LONG DO COPYRIGHTS LAST?

In Canada, the general term of copyright in a work is the entire life of the last surviving co-author plus fifty years after their death. In most countries, this term is the entire life plus seventy years. If the work has been co-authored by several people, the term of protection will last for the entire term of their lives until the last co-author dies. From that moment on, you'll count either fifty or seventy years. After that period has expired, then the work will fall into the public domain when anybody can use it without asking permission.

Subject to several special cases, performances are protected for 50 years after the end of the calendar year in which the performance took place. Sound recordings are protected for 50 years after the end of the calendar year in which the sound recording was made. Broadcasts are protected for 50 years after the end of the calendar year in which the communication signal was broadcast.

WHERE ARE COPYRIGHTS PROTECTED?

Not only are your works, performances, sound recordings, and broadcasts protected automatically upon their creation, they are automatically protected worldwide (with a few insignificant exceptions) because of the international treaties to which most countries are parties.

> **Copyright protection is automatic and worldwide.**

If you create the work in Canada, it will be automatically recognized pretty much everywhere else in the world. Also, if you steal material from somebody who lives in Pakistan, they can still sue you wherever you are using it, and they don't need to do anything to acquire that extra-territorial protection.

Likewise, most countries are parties to international treaties that provide protection to performances, sound recordings, and broadcasts originating from other countries. Again, there are a few exceptions, but for all practical purposes, they are mostly irrelevant.

Unlike most other areas of IP, no initial investment is necessary to give you protection worldwide. The combination of automatic and worldwide protection makes copyright a very powerful tool that you can use and that can be used against you. Use it wisely and be careful!

MORAL RIGHTS

Unlike the economic rights to exploit the copyright in a work, the "ownership" or entitlement to moral rights cannot be transferred in an agreement. Moral rights stay with the author—even if they have transferred ownership of the economic rights in his work. Moral rights vary from country to country. In Canada, for example, authors of all works, even a business document, have moral rights in their works (which are waivable). In other countries, such as the United States, only fine artists have moral rights in their creations. In Europe, moral rights are not only not transferrable, they cannot even be waived.

Beware of moral rights.

In some countries, moral rights are the same duration as the economic rights, some expire upon death of the author, and yet in other countries moral rights are perpetual, even after the expiry of copyright.

The right of integrity is one moral right. This is the right to modify or to allow others to modify a work. Generally when you run a website, you will want the right to modify it and although this may be an economic right (the right to create derivative works and the right to modify / alter the work), it may also relate to the moral right of integrity. In this situation, it is best to get a waiver of this moral right (where waivers are permitted) and be able to make any modifications to the site internally or with the help of another designer.

Another moral right is the right of paternity, which is the right to be identified as the work's author by name, under a pseudonym, or anonymously. If you prefer not to give credit to the designer, you should agree on this in writing. There is no right and wrong route, but it is an issue that you need to resolve with the designer before you agree to hire him.

PRE-EXISTING MATERIALS AND THIRD-PARTY CONTENT

Just because your web designer can find some nice images on Google, does not mean that you can use them on your website. Just because you can see how JavaScript works to create an interactive experience on other websites, does not mean you can simply copy it.

Unauthorized use of images, scripts, commercial fonts or content will likely infringe copyright of someone who created them. And it is your responsibility to make sure you don't use unauthorized content in your business because if you become successful, it is your coaching business (and maybe even you personally), not the web designer, that will be sued if the copyright owner decides that you have enough money to go after.

Your contract with the designer should include a provision that would disallow the use of third-party content other than with your prior approval.

It should also contain indemnification provisions. In other words, the designer must undertake to compensate you for any losses that you may incur if you get sued by someone whose works the designer used for your website.

Business owners often face a difficult dilemma: the amount at stake does not justify spending a fortune on having a lawyer draft that perfect agreement that will ideally fit a specific set of facts, yet the free templates available on the internet leave out too many important details or may be governed by laws of a different jurisdiction. In these circumstances, all too often, business owners opt for having no agreements at all.

I really wanted to help businesses bridge the gap between these two extremes, so I decided to offer simplified templates for agreements that address most of the issues that usually arise in generic situations. These templates are the result of almost twenty years of hands-on experience drafting customized contracts for hundreds of clients.

So I made these templates available for you to download from *http://NiceContracts.com* at a fraction of the cost that I charge for the customized versions. These templates cover about 85 percent of what goes into a customized agreement. In fact, I use these templates to draft customized agreements for my clients—they are *that* good. Yet they cost about ten to twenty times less than the customized ones.

If you can't afford a lawyer to draft a custom agreement for your particular situation, then at least start with a good template. Don't just rely on stuff that you can easily find on the web because most of the time, these templates miss out on a lot of important issues and are governed by U.S. law. American copyright law does not generally recognize moral rights and it has the concept of "deemed works-for-hire", which significantly changes how you approach your independent contractors compared to Canada (or pretty much the rest of the world). Even if your business is in the United States, you want to make sure you can safely expand to countries where moral rights are addressed differently.

While *some* agreement is better than nothing most of the time, it's still likely not good enough.

A different side of the same issue is when you enter into a contract with a company, rather than an individual. You need to make sure that the company has properly contracted with everyone who is going to take part in the development of your web design. These may be employees, independent contractors or outsourced force. The goal is to make sure that the company indemnifies you if you are sued by these individuals claiming that they have not properly transferred their copyright to the company that you contracted with.

> **Your contract with the designer should contain a provision disallowing the use of third-party content without your approval.**

Remember, you cannot tell the copyright owner to sue the party that you dealt with. It is you (or your company) that is using the work without permission. It is you (or your company) that will get sued. All you can do is request compensation from the party that you dealt with. This is one of the few problems with outsourcing work to someone in distant jurisdictions. If you get sued, it is very unlikely that you will be able to recover your money from someone in Pakistan whom you have never met.

The same applies to content that your designer or copywriter may have created in the past.

Very rarely will you hire someone who has never created anything in their life before they met you. Most likely, they will have done enough to impress you with their portfolio.

What this means is that there must be other clients (hopefully) happy with what your designer or copywriter has done for them. They key words here are "for them."

You want to make sure that your content creator does not sell you something he has already sold to someone else. At the very least, you want to *know* what previously created works your content creator is including in what he creates for you.

The solution, of course, is to have an agreement in writing which should clearly state that the creator must not use any materials other than:

1| original materials specifically created for you pursuant to the agreement;

2| materials that you yourself may provide to the contractor / employee;

3| pre-existing materials created by your contractor / employee but only if you have approved each such use; and

4| third-party materials but only if the contractor / employee can secure consent of the third party *and* if you have approved each such use.

Of course, this applies not only to your website but to any kind of content you have others create for you.

The template for the Content Creation Agreement takes care of these and many other issues. Get it at *http://NiceContracts.com*.

SO WHAT SHOULD THE CONTRACT SAY?

You should insist that the copyright in everything that you are paying to create be assigned to you. This way, you will become the new owner of the copyright and will own your content outright. There are situations when an exclusive license will do, but it's rarely the case when you are hiring someone to create something specifically for you. There is no reason why designers, copywriters, and other content creators should retain ownership of the content they would not have created unless you asked and paid them to do it.

Whether your agreement with your designer results in all copyrights in your website being transferred to you (assignment) or in these rights being controlled by you through a license agreement, you will want de facto exclusive rights to your website design. In your contract, therefore, you should make sure the designer agrees not to reuse the materials he created for your website for others. Otherwise, you may end up dealing with your competitors using a very similar design.

This is also something to consider when reviewing the use of third-party material in your website. If you do decide to use third-party content, you should decide, when clearing the rights to use it, whether you also need to require exclusive rights to this material. For example, if the third-party material is a photograph, would you be happy if this photograph were to appear on a competitor's website as well?

Even though assignment of copyright implies that you have the entire scope of rights with respect to the content, it's still a good idea to expressly state that you will own the right to modify and alter that content and create derivative works therefrom without having to seek the author's consent.

You should be able to take some elements of the content (paragraphs from copy, elements of website layout, etc.) and use them as you see fit. You should be able to use these elements in a different context. Do you have the right to use these works in a different manner or form? What does your agreement state about making derivative works? You may want to use some of the website's interface features (colors, fonts, and images) as part of your offline marketing materials (brochures, booklets, business cards).

You may also want to use elements of the design as a trademark. You may want to maintain the right to do these things without obtaining permission from the designer who created your website. Add this to your checklist of clauses to your designer's agreement.

Otherwise, you may find yourself hostage to a difficult dilemma— either to continue using the services of your initial designer forever or to be forced to redesign the whole website and derivative materials from scratch.

> **Avoid having to choose between using the services of the same designer forever or redesigning the whole website from scratch.**

Another issue in this respect is whether you will be required to indicate the designer's name as the author of the design. There is no right and wrong answer here, but it is certainly an issue that you need to resolve with the designer before you agree to hire him or her.

So, let's recap:

1| Always have your agreements with the designer in writing (preferably, in hardcopy or at least electronically);

2| Make sure the contract properly identifies the other party (is it an individual, a company, a partnership? the party's full name and address? if the other party is an individual, consider taking a copy of their ID);

3| Make sure you own the right to what you are paying for;

4| Make sure the designer undertakes not to create copies of your website for others;

5| Make sure the designer undertakes not to use third-party materials (including images, scripts and fonts) unless you OK each such use;

6| Make sure the contract contains a provision that will allow you to recover your losses from the designer if you are sued by a third party whose materials the designer used without your approval;

7| If you are entering into a contract with a company, make sure the company indemnifies you if you are sued by the company's own disgruntled employees or contractors;

8| Make sure you have the right to make modifications to the website without having to hire the same designer and without having to seek the original designer's consent;

9| Make sure you have the right to use materials used in the website in your offline marketing materials without having to hire the same designer.

10| Make sure to settle the issue of whether you should identify the name of the designer on your website and marketing materials.

If a designer that you are planning to hire, or a web design company or a design crowdsourcing website, refuses to address these issues in a formal agreement, think twice about dealing with them. You need to decide whether it is a good idea to put yourself in the position of paying for the privilege of being held hostage by the designer's whim.

> **If the designer refuses to address important issues in a formal agreement, run away!**

A thorough agreement drafted by an experienced copyright lawyer will cover all of these and many other issues. You see, the negotiation process tends to go much smoother before any work has been done and before the money has changed hands. Typically, the cost of helping parties resolve a dispute is much higher than the cost of preventing it by proactively answering all the "*what ifs*" and "*how comes*" in the text of a contract. That's in addition to the indirect costs of the time wasted on unproductive activities rather than what brings you pleasure or generates money.

RELEASES

People have rights. People whose photos, videos, and testimonials you use to promote your coaching business have rights.

At the very least, you should be absolutely sure that every single person whose face, voice, or thoughts you are going to use to promote your coaching business are OK with that.

Much better if you can get them to acknowledge it in a way you can document.

In many cases, a video of the person confirming that they give permission to use the recording by any means, including for the purposes of promoting your establishment, would suffice. This is how you do simple video testimonials: you ask them on camera to identify themselves and then you ask them if they give you permission to use the video in your marketing materials. And then you record the actual testimonial.

Ideally, you want a signed release that will detail what, where and for how long you can do with the photo or recording, and for what purposes. You want them to confirm that they release and discharge you from any claims that may result out of your use of the recording, including all claims based upon invasion of privacy, right of publicity, defamation, infringement of copyright, or violation of any other right.

> **Ideally, you want a signed release.**

RISK MANAGEMENT

Law, and intellectual property law is no different, is all about risk management.

It's not about whether an activity is legal or illegal, it's about the risk of certain negative consequences occurring as a result of the activity.

> **Law is about risk management.**

If you've decided to use some content that is not yours, there are three questions you should ask.

- If somebody finds out about it, what are the chances they will do something about it?

- If they decide to do something about it, what are the chances that they will win?

- If they win, what's the worst thing that can happen to me?

If you realize that the chances of getting caught are high and the potential consequences are very serious, you will probably stop using that content without asking permission.

If both the consequences and the risk are small, then, while what you're doing may still not be perfectly legal, it wouldn't be the first thing you would fix in your business. There are always other important things to be done first.

Please recognize that I'm not advocating infringement of others' IP. I certainly am not encouraging that you violate the law. However, from a practical perspective, I understand that seldom will you be able to have everything perfect at all times, and IP is no exception.

Now, if you ask a lawyer about intellectual property, the proper response would be, "*Yes, you need to get all those licenses and permissions for it to be perfectly legal.*" Why do they say that? Because they need to protect themselves from lawsuits.

However, just because something is perfectly legal doesn't necessarily mean that it's perfectly advisable in your particular situation. Sometimes, people whose rights you may be infringing simply don't care.

Having said that, when you get caught using someone's intellectual property without permission, you need to deal with the consequences. And the first thing you need to do is answer these questions:

- What do I do now?

- Do I just take it down and wait to see what they do?

- Do I simply pay them what they're asking me to pay?

- What are the odds that they're going to use me as an example and take me to court?

- If they do take me to court, how much money will the judge award them?

- Will it be worth it for them to take me to court?

- Will it be worth it for me to try and defend myself in court?

Figuring out the answers to these questions still largely falls under risk management. Unless the amounts at stake are significant, in most cases, nobody is going to take you to court. But…they may. That's the risk you take.

Whenever you set up a business, the main question you need to address is, "What is it that I need to do to make sure that if somebody comes after me, my business still survives?" You don't have to be 100 percent bulletproof because that is going to take a lot of money, but you need to protect the foundations of your business. This is why it is crucial that you understand your IP strategy.

But remember this about the law, and intellectual property law in particular, it's always about figuring out if the potential reward is worth the cost of getting there.

The issue of risk management is what should drive your decisions about the degree of sophistication in your contracts, whether to get a written release from your clients when they leave a testimonial, when to get a license to use images used on your website, etc.

It's your risk. Manage it responsibly.

BE CAREFUL MONETIZING YOUR OWN CONTENT

Few things are more powerful than a contract. Contracts can create and destroy rights and obligations, overriding default provisions contained in most laws. No matter what steps you have taken to protect your IP, if you sign a bad contract that deals with your intellectual property, you may be in for a big surprise about how the status quo has just changed. Oh, and sometimes you will be deemed to have entered into a contract without signing anything. Simply because you did something, such as responding *"OK"* by email or clicking the *"I ACCEPT"* button, may mean you have entered into a contract with someone.

I had a client who was a book writer. He was paranoid about registering his copyrights. He was writing a book, and for some unknown reason, he thought it was a good idea to obtain a new copyright registration certificate every single time he finished writing a new chapter. By the time he had finished the whole thing, he had a big stack of copyright certificates.

Ironically, a few days after he had received the final registration certificate for the entire book, he met with a publisher in a restaurant. The publisher told the writer how much he loved the book and that he really-really-really wanted to publish it. He even brought a standard agreement with him. *"Here, see, it says that you will be paid a hefty 30% of the publisher's revenue from each book sold. This is way more than the usual practice, but this book is amazing, and I want to make sure I get this deal."*

The writer could not contain his smile. Life has just gotten better. Finally someone has recognized his superior ability to write great books. And here he was, just a few days after typing the last paragraph of the last chapter, signing an amazing contract with this charming publisher. He signed.

And waited.

And waited some more.

A year later, the writer found out that a film company was making a movie based on his book.

He called the movie company and inquired how come nobody told him that a movie would be made based on his book, and more importantly where was his money?! The movie company told the writer that they had purchased all necessary rights from the publisher and that they were very sorry but they had no obligation to pay anything.

Then he called the publisher. The publisher told him that according to the contract, the writer had assigned all of his rights in the book in exchange for 30% of the publisher's revenue from each book sold. But you see, the publisher had no revenue from books sold because the publisher never published any books. In fact, the publisher never intended to publish the book. The publisher merely resold the rights to the movie company. The publisher was, of course, very sorry, but he had no obligation to pay the writer. Not until some books were sold.

This is when the writer came to see me. He brought with him all of his copyright certificates, carrying them as if he was holding a priceless treasure, or at least a priceless treasure map. Matter-of-factly, he also produced the copy of his agreement with the publisher—as if it was a meaningless piece of paper.

When I read the contract and told him that his registration certificates on which he spent well over a thousand dollars were worthless, it was a tough pill to swallow. He just could not fathom how a simple contract could override his copyrights.

But this is the nature of contracts. This is their very purpose—to change the status quo by creating and destroying rights.

The transfer of copyright rendered copyright registrations in the writer's name worthless. And failure of the writer to foresee that he was giving away his rights for free destroyed his ability to make any money off the book he tried so hard to protect.

The moral of the story: be very careful about allowing others to use your IP—whether you do it through a written agreement or not.

TIPS & TRICKS

In addition to getting the templates you can use to document the transfer of IP from your contractors at ***http://NiceContracts.com***, there are a number of things you should do to ensure your content becomes your asset, not your Achilles' heel.

KEEP DRAFTS

First of all, always keep drafts and backups of everything you create. This is the best way to provide evidence that you created the material because you can demonstrate the developmental process you have gone through to create it.

COPYRIGHT NOTICES

You should use a copyright notice on the copies of your content. A copyright notice is typically a "C" in a circle (©) followed by year of the first publication, followed by the name of the copyright owner.

For example, the copyright notice for this book is, **©2013–2015 by Andrei Mincov and Trademark Factory International Inc.,** which means that this book was written between 2013 and 2015 and is currently owned by me and my company. And no, you have no way of knowing about the arrangement that I have with my company as to who owns what.

The copyright symbol is not found on standard keyboards. If you are using Windows, hold down the ALT key followed by 0169, or simply hit CTRL + ALT + C in Microsoft Word.

POOR MAN'S COPYRIGHT

A poor man's copyright is when you put your work in an envelope, seal it, and then mail it to yourself. Admittedly, there are many flaws in this from the perspective of evidence because nothing prevents you from doing some switching in the process. This method is not perfect by far. But it's better than nothing at all.

You can also email yourself the material but this is even weaker than mailing it to yourself because it's fairly easy to tinker with the headers, dates, and times in any email message.

On the other hand, remember the story about the two guys who were out in the woods when suddenly a grizzly charged them? As the bear was gaining on them, one man stopped and began to put on a pair of running shoes. The second man stops beside him and says, "*Are you crazy? The bear is too fast for us. You don't think those running shoes will help you outrun the bear, do you?*" The first man replies, "*Don't need to. All I have to do is outrun you.*"

Your goal in a courtroom is not to have the best evidence in the world. Your goal is to have evidence that is better than the evidence of the other party. And the evidence in the form of poor man's copyright could be just enough to help you win.

COPYRIGHT REGISTRATION

Because copyright does not protect underlying ideas, only how these ideas are actually expressed in a sequence of words or images, typically, coaches don't have much content worthy of a registered copyright.

But there are exceptions. The most notable ones are books and courses sold on tangible media or online. Granted, the only reason these are exceptions is because they are examples of going beyond what is expected of a typical coach. But again, we're not talking about faceless trainers. We're talking about those who want to be legendary.

What are you going to leave behind?

Copyright registration doesn't create protection—copyright protection is automatic by virtue of you having created the work. What it does do is add certain presumptions and remedies that you can use if you see that somebody is infringing on your right.

Registration in Canada is very peculiar because, unlike in the States, in Canada, you don't deposit the work that you want to register. All you do is notify the Canadian Intellectual Property Office that you have created a work that has a certain title and that you want that title to be registered in your name in Canada. If you put together a personal development book and call it "Wake Up One Hour Early and Conquer Yourself", that's what you're going to tell them: *"This is a book that I wrote. It's called 'Wake Up One Hour Early and Conquer Yourself'. Here's your 50 dollars."* You then get a certificate of registration. In my opinion, this is a big flaw in Canada's system of registration because it doesn't really provide any information to anyone about what the work really is.

In the United States, when you file for copyright registration, you are required to submit the work itself, and they will look into it and make sure that it's proper subject matter for registration. This allows people to have a reference point to compare their material with any material that has been copyrighted by someone else.

Interestingly, the fees are lower in the U.S. (US$35 compared to CA$50), so I always recommend to my clients who have decided to register copyright that they register both in Canada and the U.S. because Canadian registration will give them certain procedural advantages if they were to have a dispute resolved in a Canadian court, but a U.S. registration will provide the proper evidence to confirm that on a certain date the work existed and that the owner claimed ownership in that work.

PROTECTING YOUR SECRETS

ONE PARAGRAPH SUMMARY

If you want others to keep your secrets secret, you should keep them secret yourself. Just like you can't stuff toothpaste back in the tube, once a secret is broken, it's no longer a secret. Use proper non-disclosure agreements when sharing your secrets with others. A good starting point is the templates you can get at *http://NiceContracts.com.*

WHAT'S YOUR SECRET SAUCE?

Let's face it—you chose a very competitive industry. The only way you will become truly successful is if you convince enough people that you know something that others in your industry don't.

This will be accomplished by clever branding, compelling content, and the air of mystery that urges your prospects to listen to you.

You already know you should be protecting your brand through trademarks.

You already know you should be protecting your content through copyright. You also learned that copyright will not protect the underlying ideas in your content, only the form in which the content was expressed.

If copyright can't protect the substance of what you teach or coach on, how do you protect your professional secrets and your proprietary information?

Say hello to trade secrets.

Throughout this book, I've done my best to keep examples relevant to the coaching industry. The only reason I am about to make an exception is because the recipe for Coca-Cola is probably the most famous example of a trade secret.

Coca-Cola patented its original recipe in 1893. We'll briefly discuss patents later in this chapter, but for now all you need to know is that it gave Coca-Cola a very short monopoly (less than 20 years), in exchange for which they had to make their original formula public knowledge.

When the recipe was changed, the company decided not to patent the formula again, choosing instead to keep it a secret. This way, the formula is not disclosed to the public, including Coca-Cola's competitors, and the protection does not expire with the expiration of the patent. Today, the formula is stored in a fancy vault. In fact, Coca-Cola has made its trade secrets one of its strongest marketing weapons.

People are conditioned to value something that is secret more than what is readily available to them. When they are told that the carbonated soft drink that they buy is actually made using a secret recipe that the company spent millions and millions of dollars protecting, they automatically attribute extra value to what they drink.

People love secrets. That's why there are so many self-development books that use the word "secret" in their title. An Amazon search for "secret" reveals 1,791 books in "Success Self-Help" category alone! If secrets are so powerful, it means that you should be protecting yours.

However, not every secret is a protectable trade secret. Trade secrets protect know-how, confidential information, and any other information that has actual or potential commercial value as a result of it being unknown to others. Pretty much anything can be a trade secret—coaching techniques, customer lists, business processes and systems, business plans, data related to sales performance of key sales personnel, phone sales scripts, checklists, internal policies, even new inventions for which you haven't filed a patent application.

> **Pretty much anything can be a trade secret, as long as it has actual or potential commercial value and is not known to others.**

As you can see, virtually anything that gives you some sort of a competitive advantage *because* you keep it confidential can be a trade secret. I'll use the example of a recipe in this chapter, but the approach is no different for your customer lists or business processes.

There are four basic requirements for something to be defined as a trade secret:

1| your secret must have actual or potential commercial value;

2| it must be well defined;

3| it must not be publicly known; and

4| it must be kept secret by the owner.

I'll go through these requirements in order.

> This book is not a comprehensive textbook on trade secrets. It only contains information directly relevant to coaches and consultants.
>
> For a more detailed (yet still in plain English) overview of trade secrets law, download my ebook *The Ultimate Insider's Guide to Trade Secrets*, a chapter from my best-selling book, *The Ultimate Insider's Guide to Intellectual Property* as part of your bonus package at *http://FacelessToLegendary.com/bonus.*

ACTUAL OR POTENTIAL COMMERCIAL VALUE

Not all secrets are trade secrets.

If you eat chocolate ice cream before going to bed and keep this away from your spouse or your fitness trainer, most likely this secret is of no commercial value—either to yourself or to anyone who might somehow find out about it. The only exception would be if you somehow discovered that eating chocolate ice cream before going to bed does something uniquely positive to your business.

Just to be clear, secrets about bad things you may have done, even if they are capable of destroying you and your business if revealed, are still not trade secrets because your knowledge of the secret does not add anything to your bottom line.

Coca-Cola makes money selling carbonated soft drinks using their particular formula, and a huge chunk of that money comes from it being able to claim that no one else has the same recipe. This secret has actual commercial value.

Imagine that you have developed a brilliant marketing strategy for your coaching business which, if implemented, will give you a tremendous competitive advantage. And imagine that if your wealthier competitor figures it out and starts using it as well, then you will lose a ton of money. This secret has potential commercial value.

WELL DEFINED

In order for something to be protected as a trade secret, it needs to be well defined. If you accuse someone of stealing your trade secret, you need to be able to explain exactly what it is and also explain to the judge that whoever stole your secret knew that it was your secret.

If you are entering into agreements with third parties, the information about what needs to be kept confidential has to be specific and detailed.

The trade secret can be difficult to define in a non-disclosure agreement without disclosing the secret itself, but unless you can do that in some measure, your non-disclosure agreement will be very weak.

For example, you can't simply state that, *"Whatever I'm going to tell you, you promise to keep confidential."* It won't work because if the recipient really discloses something and then you try to enforce the agreement, no court in the world is going to agree with you that the recipient really understood what they were supposed to keep secret. At the very least, you have to define the area of knowledge that pertains to the trade secret. As in, *"I am going to share with you the secret strategy we use to close 28% of the room when we do our free 2-hour workshops. You must keep it confidential."*

You must describe the subject matter of your trade secret with sufficient detail to separate it from matters of general knowledge, and to permit the recipients of your confidential information to ascertain at least the boundaries within which the secret lies.

NOT PUBLICLY KNOWN

This one should be fairly obvious. If something is already publicly known, then it can't be a trade secret. It also means that if someone does figure out your secret (through legal means) then you can no longer claim it as your trade secret.

For example, if you were somehow able to figure out the recipe for Coca-Cola and you did this without breaking into their vault or breaching a contract, then nothing stops you from sharing this information with the public. Once the information becomes publicly known, the recipe is no longer a trade secret.

Essentially, there are three ways your secret can become publicly known without anybody violating your rights: you may deliberately choose to disclose the secret to the public, you may fail to take proper steps to keep your secret confidential, or someone may simply figure it out independently.

Either way, just as you can't put toothpaste back in the tube, once your secret is out, it's no longer a secret. You have no one else to blame but yourself.

Of course, the toughest pill to swallow is when somebody figures out your secret on their own. It's not unusual for us to overestimate our ability to create something unique. Whenever you are choosing to protect something through a trade secret as part of your IP strategy, ask yourself—and be brutally honest—"How difficult would it be for my competitors to figure out what my secret is if they were to analyze my products and services with a fine-tooth comb?"

Would another experienced marketer be able to crack your secret close-28%-of-the-room strategy? What if they sat through your presentation and recorded your every word?

Don't rely on trade secret protection unless you are sure that your secret is not easily breakable.

KEPT SECRET BY THE OWNER

Keeping something secret doesn't simply mean that the owner of the trade secret should refuse to share the secret with anyone. The owner has to take clear, specific steps to ensure that the secret is kept secret. This means you need to keep things locked up, you need to have employees sign confidentiality agreements and whatever else you can do to show that you are actively trying to keep your secret safe.

That's why attendees of experienced training companies and coaches won't be allowed to enter the room unless they sign a release or a contract that contains a promise not to use or disclose confidential information that will be disclosed to the attendee during the event.

If you have all your secret documents lying around in your office and a cleaning lady comes by and sees those documents, takes a photograph, and publishes them on Facebook, that's it. It's no longer a secret because you didn't have a confidentiality agreement with employees, and you didn't take proper steps to keep those documents secret.

If the defendant can prove that you didn't really care to keep your secret confidential, the judge will have very little sympathy for you.

Judges often decide cases based on who has a better story and who is more believable. Trade secrets is one of the areas where creating the better story is essential. A story about your competitor breaking into your office in a ninja suit through a window on the twenty-eighth floor is very different from a story about your competitor readily spotting your secret in a pile of documents carelessly scattered around your desk while in a business meeting with you.

WHERE ARE TRADE SECRETS PROTECTED?

The territory covered by trade secrets is essentially any country which recognizes your right to protect your confidential information. Most countries protect confidential information in some shape or form, but some of them have specific requirements that you must follow.

For example, a country might require you to mark every page of your confidential materials with a stamp saying, *Confidential Information*. If you don't do this, then it might no longer be considered to be a trade secret.

So you should look into the confidentiality requirements for each country where you are interested in protecting your information.

HOW LONG DOES TRADE SECRET PROTECTION LAST?

In theory, trade secrets can be protected for as long as the information remains unknown to the public while still being of actual or potential commercial value.

In practice, of course, very few secrets can truly stand the test of time. With time, either the secret is leaked, or the protected information simply becomes irrelevant.

What's important is that the secret serves you and your business for as long as it continues to provide you with a competitive advantage.

SO HOW DO TRADE SECRETS PROTECT YOU?

No one who receives access to your trade secrets through an agreement with you is allowed to violate the terms of that agreement. The agreement usually includes an obligation not to use or further disclose your trade secrets other than as specified in the contract.

Let's say you trained your assistant (who had, of course, signed an agreement containing a non-disclosure clause) to handle prospects from the moment they first sign up to receive your email newsletter all the way up to the point when the prospect runs to the back of the room with a credit card. So if she quit and founded her own training company, then you can take action against your ex-assistant if she starts using *your* secret to replicate your process in her new business. You won't be able to prevent her from competing with you, but you can and *should* make sure that she is not competing with you using your own trade secrets.

If you shared your trade secret with an investor and had him sign a non-disclosure agreement (NDA), and the investor blabs about it on his blog, then you can take action against that investor for disclosing your trade secrets.

Bottom line is, you can only take action against someone who received your trade secrets and only if you can show that this person knew or should have known that disclosing the information was in violation of the recipient's confidentiality obligations.

For example, if Company A discloses some information to Company B under an NDA, then Company A can enforce the terms of the non-disclosure agreement against Company B if Company B discloses that information to Company C.

However, it would be very difficult for Company A to go after Company C because Company C did not promise anything to Company A. In legal terms, this is called *privity of contract*. This concept limits your ability to enforce contracts to only those who entered into a contractual relationship with you. With trade secrets, you can take it one step further and enforce the confidentiality regime against Company C, but only if you can prove that Company C knew or must have known that the disclosure by Company B would be in breach of its obligations to Company A.

This is usually a difficult thing to prove since Company C could simply claim that they thought it was okay for Company B to give them the information. In this scenario, you are back to square one and your only remedy would be to go after Company B. If Company B has no money to pay you for your losses, you're out of luck.

A properly drafted non-disclosure agreement should cover more than just non-disclosure. A very important part of these agreements is *non-use*.

> **A properly drafted non-disclosure agreement should also cover non-use.**

Let's say, you came up with an amazing system that teaches first-time entrepreneurs how to make their first $500,000 within 5 months, guaranteed. You've had a great deal of success with it and now you want to license it out to another coaching company for a good payout. So you meet with that other company's CEO and have him sign an NDA according to which you will disclose your secret strategy. Not only do you want to make sure that the competitor does not disseminate your secret further, you also want to make sure that they don't actually teach their students your strategy—unless you get paid.

A good NDA would cover the following aspects:

- define the secret;

- confirm that the secret is being disclosed to the recipient;

- state the purposes for the disclosure;

- explain the expectations of the disclosing party in disclosing the secret;

- set limits to how the recipient is allowed to use the secret;

- explicitly list what the recipient is not allowed to do with the secret (usually non-use, non-disclosure, and non-competition); and

- clearly state the negative consequences that the recipient will face if the recipient chooses to breach the contract.

You can download a template of a one-way Non-Disclosure Agreement at *http://NiceContracts.com*. This template covers situations when you are about to disclose some confidential information to someone else for a particular purpose, and need to make sure that this information will remain confidential. You are not assuming any obligations of confidentiality, just the recipient of your confidential information.

Think of trade secrets as a combination of *what you do* and *what contracts you enter into*?

As you can see, the *"what you do"* part is about you taking steps to protect your secrets (such as not leaving your secret files in open view). If you don't do certain things, you won't have anything left to protect.

The *contracts you enter into* is *how* you are protecting your secret. The protection will really only be as good as your contract. If your contract only says that the recipient can't disclose the secret but leaves out the issue of whether the recipient can implement your secret, it is unlikely that you would be able to prevent the recipient from using your secret if the recipient diligently prevents your secret from further disclosure.

Now, let's assume you've taken all the right steps to establish that you have a trade secret, and you've entered into all the right contracts to define how your secrets are to be treated by others. What if the contract is breached?

Your remedies would be an injunction (when the judge orders the recipient to stop using or disclosing the trade secret) and damages (when the judge orders that the recipient—or a third party, if you're lucky—pay you money).

It is prudent to identify the measure of your potential losses in the non-disclosure agreement in case of breach. For example, if you specify sanctions in the contract, and the recipient still chooses to violate the contract, you will have a much easier argument in court as to why your secret is worth a billion dollars. But be careful. In most countries, you can't implement penalties for breach of contract into your agreement. The idea is that you are not supposed to benefit from someone violating the terms of the contract. In other words, you cannot end up better off if someone chooses to breach the contract compared to if he chose to follow it to a T.

TIPS & TRICKS

There are a number of tips and tricks to ensure that your trade secrets will remain secret and be recognized by the courts as such.

KEEP IT SECRET

This should be pretty obvious. If you have something that you don't want other people to have access to, to disclose, or to use, take measures to restrict access to your secrets, and make sure that whoever has access to your secrets *"knows their limit and plays within it."*

Of course, the best way to protect your secret is to not share it with anybody at all, but this may not be practical if you want to implement the secret and make money.

MAKE YOUR EMPLOYEES KEEP IT SECRET

You need to ensure that your employees and independent contractors all sign agreements stating that they won't disclose your (well-defined) secrets to anybody.

You should have policies that govern what can and cannot be disclosed and how your confidential information can be used. You should have clear guidelines for employees reflected in your employment agreements and employee manuals.

It is also crucial that you have a social-media policy covering anyone who comes in contact with your business. Make sure your employees fully understand that it is inappropriate to tweet certain things that may seem like mundane updates to an employee but are, in fact, trade secrets of the company.

You may remember the tragic story of Connor Riley, who was really happy that she was offered a well-paying job at Cisco, but she was still weighing all the pros and cons of accepting it.

She summoned the wisdom of the internet and tweeted: *"Cisco just offered me a job! Now I have to weigh the utility of a fatty paycheck against the daily commute to San Jose and hating work.*"

Twitter really helped her solve this dilemma because guess who didn't get the job?

One of Cisco's high-ranking employees tweeted back: "*Who is the hiring manager? I'm sure they would love to know you will hate the work. We here at Cisco are versed in the web.*"

USE NON-DISCLOSURE AGREEMENTS (NDAS)

Whenever you can, make sure that whoever you disclose your trade secrets to signs a non-disclosure agreement with you. The general rule is simple: the higher the risk, the more detailed your NDA should be.

For a template of a professionally drafted non-disclosure agreement, check out ***http://NiceContracts.com***.

Just like with any other type of contracts, NDAs are about "who wants whom more."

The more valuable the thing you have to offer, the easier it will be for you to convince others to sign whatever you want them to sign.

It's easy to get your employees to sign NDAs. They want the job, so they will sign the contract. If they don't sign the contract, they don't get the job. Easy.

When it comes to talking to investors, you will have to walk a bit of a tightrope. Most investors will not want to sign an NDA until they know enough about the secret to pique their interest. You will have to disclose just enough information to hook them and then bring up signing an NDA if they want to learn more. The trick is figuring out how much is enough and how much is too much.

Investors are now very careful about signing NDAs unless they are

100 percent sure that the information you disclose to them will not relate in some way to what they have already been working on. Signing the NDA might jeopardize the investor's ability to continue working on something that is being developed without your trade secrets. The investor surely does not want to let you claim that if not for your secret, the investor would never have gotten the results that he did.

So your goal is to make them want you more than you want them. You need to figure out a way to tell them as little as possible but still have them drooling to learn more about the rest of your secret. This is when you pull out your NDA and say, *"Please sign on the dotted line."*

If all you can tell the investor is, *"I think I came up with a great way for you to make a lot of money, but I can't tell you until you sign this document right here,"* don't expect to walk away with a signed NDA. In fact, it would be a miracle if the investor even deigned to explain to you why he would never, ever, sign such a document.

WHAT IF YOU CAME UP WITH SOMETHING GROUNDBREAKING?

The only way to protect some inventions is to patent them.

Let's say you invented a gadget that analyzes people's brain waves and automatically generates the perfect 3-year plan for their personal life and their business.

Should you patent it? Can you patent it?

There are three big challenges with patenting. First, the requirements to get something patented are extremely burdensome. Second, patenting is extremely expensive. Third, a patent only protects you for a very short period—less than twenty years.

LET'S START WITH THE REQUIREMENTS.

First of all, your invention must not have been made public by anyone, anywhere. This is what the law means when it says that in order to be patentable, the invention must be *new*. Even if it's your own invention, with a few limited exceptions, you are still not allowed to disclose it to the public until you have filed for the patent.

> **For an invention to be patentable, it must be new, useful, and non-obvious.**

Disclosing doesn't just mean publishing in a scientific magazine. It means providing enough information for those sophisticated in the area of knowledge to which your invention pertains that they will be able to understand the substance of your invention.

This may include selling your gadget or even writing an article on your blog about your new technology that prints food.

If you share your invention with an investor under a non-disclosure agreement, and the investor keeps it to himself, it does not count as a public disclosure and would not hurt your chances of getting your invention patented.

But once the information is out there, even if the inventor is the source of the disclosure, the invention is no longer new.

When I say, "out there", I mean "out there *anywhere*". Even if you only make your gadget available in a single store in a small village in Moldova, this may be enough to destroy your chances of getting a patent—not just in Moldova but anywhere in the world.

The second requirement is that the invention must be *useful*. This doesn't really mean that your invention has to be of some particular use to anybody. It just means that your invention has to provide at least some identifiable benefit and that it is capable of being made and used by anyone who saw your patent and is somewhat knowledgeable in your industry.

In the United States, this requirement is referred to as "utility", hence the term "utility patent" being used in the States. The invention must do something.

In Europe, this requirement has the form of an "industrial applicability" test, which is slightly different but still reflects a similar idea—there must be something about the invention that would make it capable of being reproduced over and over again with the purpose of performing a certain function or achieving a certain result.

Either way, this requirement is the easiest to meet because as long as your invention can be made and as long as it can produce some meaningful result, you meet the requirement.

Coming up with an idea that it would be great to have a brain-analyzing gadget is not enough to make your idea patentable, even if you are the first person who's ever thought about it.

This book is not a comprehensive textbook on patents. It only contains information directly relevant to coaches and consultants.

For a more detailed (yet still in plain English) overview of patent law, download my ebook *The Ultimate Insider's Guide to Patents*, a chapter from my best-selling book, *The Ultimate Insider's Guide to Intellectual Property* as part of your bonus package at ***http://FacelessToLegendary.com/bonus.***

Unless you know (and share with the Patent Office) how to actually build one and how it will work, you haven't demonstrated that your invention is useful.

"Wouldn't it be nice" is not good enough. Hypothetical devices are not patentable.

One of the underlying ideas behind the patent system is that the public should be able to use inventions after the patent expires. If the patent does not provide enough information for the public to do that, then there is very little value that the public receives in exchange for granting the monopoly to the patent owner. This is the reason why usefulness is a requirement for patent protection.

With respect to the coaching industry, you need to bear in mind that strategies that depend in their implementation on your professional expertise are usually not patentable. You can't patent a strategy if a novice coach can't figure out how to reliably master it simply by reading the patent.

Finally, the third requirement is that the invention must ***not be obvious***. It is typically the hardest to meet, and this is where a lot of tension arises between the Patent Office and the inventor.

You may have to deal with the patent examiner's objections regarding obviousness if your invention is not described in a single existing source (in which case it would not have been new) but results from combining a number of already known components.

The determination of whether an invention is obvious relies on a mythical person who knows everything that currently exists. This person knows every single patent out there, every single journal, every single magazine article, and every single blog post. The person knows everything but is totally incapable of inventing anything new even if the person's life depended on it. So the question the patent examiner asks is, *"Would this person be able to come up with what you're trying to patent?"* If the answer is yes, even a person with zero creativity could still put two and two together and come up with the same solution, then your invention is obvious, and you cannot get a patent. If our mythical person would look at what you've come up with and think, *"Wow, I'll be damned. I knew about this part and I certainly knew about that part. But I wouldn't for the life of me have thought that you could combine them to get such an amazing result,"* then your invention is non-obvious and you have managed to go over the steepest hurdle of patentability.

So let's say you came up with your brain analyzer idea and decided to patent it, and the Patent Office made a reasonable observation that brain wave scanners have been around for some time and so have career aptitude tests. Is your invention obvious?

Usually, the answer is born as a result of some back-and-forth with the Patent Office when they claim that your invention is obvious. You'll say, "Well, if this is so obvious, how come nobody has used brain wave scanners to generate business plans?" And they'll say, "Maybe they have, they just didn't do anything public with it?" And you'd say, "This is such a great idea, I'm sure that if somebody came up with it, it'd be used by business owners throughout the country!" And so on, and so on.

SHOULD YOU GET A PATENT?

Because getting and maintaining a patent is very expensive (depending on the number of countries where you a seeking a patent, we're talking from tens to hundreds of thousands of dollars), the lifespan of the patent is one of the most important considerations in deciding whether or not to get a patent.

A patent lasts for twenty years after the date of application. This is important because the clock doesn't start running once the patent is granted—it starts running as soon as you apply.

> **A patent is only good for 20 years.**

The normal amount of time it takes to get a patent is about four to six years and all of this time is counted as part of the duration of the patent. This means that you actually only have a patent for fifteen years or so.

You also need to decide if there will still be value in your invention by the time the patent is issued. If your invention is going to be obsolete before you are even granted a patent, you may decide to not bother.

Finally, you should decide if your invention will remain valuable after the patent expires. Remember, in order to get a patent, you need to disclose all the details of how to use or make your invention. If your invention is still relevant and valuable after twenty years, people will be lining up to use it and there is nothing you can do to stop them. This is precisely how the generics market works in the pharmaceutical industry. One company develops a new drug, enjoys a brief monopoly, and then it's fair game for anyone else to copy it.

There may be situations where you would be better off keeping the whole thing to yourself as a trade secret in an attempt to continue making a profit from your invention. In other words, can you make money through your invention while keeping it a secret?

Essentially the thought process should go like this:

1| Is it valuable?

2| If it is valuable, can I protect it by any means other than a patent?

3| If I can't protect it other than through a patent, is it patentable?

4| If it's patentable, is it *really-really-really* valuable?

If it's patentable and really-really-really valuable, find the money and file for the patent. Otherwise, don't bother.

So in case of your amazing brain wave crystal ball, here's how your thought process would go.

Is it valuable? Absolutely. It's going to revolutionize the coaching industry forever!

Can you protect it through a trade secret? Only if you want to restrict the use of the gadget to yourself and your licensees and franchises. In other words, you will not be selling the gadget on the open market. This can allow you to make a good deal of money in your coaching business, but it won't allow you to make money by selling the gadget to the public. If you want to keep the magic gadget to yourself, then you don't need a patent. Otherwise, trade secret protection would not be available.

Is it patentable? Assuming that your gadget actually works, yes. You have a new, non-obvious and useful invention.

Is it *really-really-really* valuable? If you had a monopoly on the fortune-telling technology for fifteen years, you'd be set for generations. So yes, it's that valuable.

If you come up with something *that* amazing, consider patenting it. But don't jump into patenting for vanity. Patents are a very peculiar area of intellectual property.

IN CONCLUSION

Today, intellectual property is not just a fancy addition to a business; it *is* the business for millions of people and businesses around the world.

If you are serious about growing your coaching business into a massive success, you owe it to yourself and everyone involved in your business to make sure that you've done everything you can to protect whatever makes you money. Look at intellectual property laws as your toolbox to build a competitive advantage. Hire your lawyers as handymen who are going to use that toolbox to help you build your dream.

> **You must protect whatever makes you money.**

Any coach or trainer who wants to transcend the faceless stage of just making enough money to stay afloat should protect his or her brand—simply because branding is what your business is about.

> Take the first step to protect your brand: order your free trademark search at *http://freeTMsearch.com*.

As a coach who hopes to become legendary, you must make sure you can withstand lawsuits from those whose content you are using. Website designers, composers, illustrators, copywriters, and so on—make sure you properly document your ownership in what you paid them to create. It'll be worth it.

If you're really successful, there's got to be something proprietary to what you do. There's got to be a reason why so many coaches go broke, and you didn't. You must have some secret ingredient to how you teach and how you do business. Protect it.

Get templates for copyright assignment, content creation and non-disclosure agreement at *http://NiceContracts.com*.

Don't forget the free bonuses you can download at *http://FacelessToLegendary.com/bonus*.

1| The Ultimate Insider's Guide to Trademarks

2| The Ultimate Insider's Guide to Copyright

3| The Ultimate Insider's Guide to Trade Secrets

4| The Ultimate Insider's Guide to Patents

5| 8 Dangerous Myths About Trademarking

6| 5 Trademarking Rip-Offs You Should Avoid

Don't settle with OK.

Say no to barely getting by.

Resist the urge to accept mediocre and faceless.

Be LEGENDARY!

MY STORY

I was been an intellectual property lawyer for most of my life.

I'm fortunate not only to love the work that I do, but also to know exactly why I love it.

Let me tell you my story.

I was born in Moscow, Russia a few years before the final whimper of the socialist Evil Empire. I became an IP lawyer when my father, Mark Minkov, a famous Russian composer who had written music for over 100 movies and a countless number of hit songs, heard his music on the radio advertising an event organized by Samsung. The problem was that nobody had asked his permission to use his music. So he called the radio station and told them that they couldn't just take his music and use it however they pleased. They told him to sit down, shut up, and be grateful because they were doing him a favour by making him even more famous.

Believe it or not, he didn't like this very much. As it often happens in Hollywood movies, he told them, "I'll see you in court!" and hung up. He was yet to figure out who would represent him in court.

You see, Russia had just adopted its first post-Soviet Copyright Act that gave authors the exclusive right to control how their works could be used by others. There were a handful of renowned Soviet-era specialists in the field of intellectual property, but their number was minuscule compared to the number of authors who were in need of their services.

At that time, I was in my second year of university majoring in international law. Russia does not divide education into undergraduate and graduate studies. After ten to twelve years of secondary school, one may attend a university, usually for four to six years. I was in my second year and, honestly, becoming a lawyer didn't really appeal to me at that time.

When my father asked me whether I could help him take this matter to court, I literally had no idea about copyright, civil procedure, or what to do in a courtroom. I still wonder what part of his request was just a test to see if I would chicken out. But I didn't throw in the towel. I said, *"Sure, let's do it!"*

Now it was my turn to figure out what to do. I asked around, read a ton of literature and found a couple of samples (and, just so you understand—you could not simply google "Copyright Lawsuit Papers". Back then, there WAS NO Google!). I finally managed to draft my very first statement of claim alleging that the radio station had infringed my father's copyright.

Then, I had to deliver the statement of claim to the judge (the process is completely different in Canada). So after sitting in line for a few hours, I finally got to see a real judge for the first time in my life. In Russia, you don't have to be called to the bar, or even have graduated from a law school, to represent clients in court. That's not to say that people weren't surprised to know that I was still a student, but no law prevented me from doing what I set out to do.

So I got to meet the judge who took my statement of claim and read all five or so pages while I was sitting across from her, in awe of her years of experience dealing with complexities of the law.

She asked me a few questions to make sure she properly understood the claim and set the date of a preliminary hearing with the defendant in attendance. Before I left, I decided to build some rapport with the judge, so I asked her a probing question, *"So, there must be a lot of copyright cases coming in with all the piracy out there?"* She responded right away, *"Yes, there are so many of them, I should probably finally read the Copyright Act."*

It was like going to a heart surgeon and asking him, *"So you must be busy these days?"* and to be told, *"Yes, there are so many patients, I should probably finally learn where the bloody heart is..."*

This was my first encounter with the Russian legal system in the 1990s. The next thing I remember was the first day of trial. It was eight in the morning, my dad was driving the car to the courthouse and my mom was in the back seat. I was in the passenger seat, wearing my best jeans and my best denim shirt, my rock-star, down-to-my-mid-back hair carefully arranged into a ponytail, with a briefcase holding the courtroom speech I had been writing until four in the morning.

The closer we got to the courthouse, the more I felt my hands shaking and my knees trembling. A feeling of absolute horror came over me. Like every good mother, my mom had a solution. She asked my dad to pull over then she rushed out to a convenience store and came back with a small bottle of vodka. She gave it to me and said, *"Here, have a drink, son!"* It was the only time I ever had a drink before trial. Then, it just brought me back to my senses.

I got to the courtroom and ripped the radio station's lawyer to shreds. I felt like a protagonist from a Chuck Norris film knocking out his opponent in the early minutes of the film. On a technicality, the other side's lawyer managed to get an adjournment (that's when the judge tells you that you're done for today and should come again on a different day).

The next day, instead of one lawyer, the radio station was represented by three. On our side, it was still me, wearing a different shirt this time. I might have been wearing the same pair of jeans. I don't really remember. I proceeded to deliver a number of knockout punches until the judge told us that she had heard enough to make a decision.

She solemnly announced that the radio station did not infringe on my dad's copyright.

I was absolutely devastated.

This is how Roy Jones Jr. must have felt when he was cheated out of the gold at the 1988 Olympics in Seoul.

When I got to read the full decision, I could not believe the nonsense I was reading. I am the first to admit when an opponent has a valid argument, but what I was reading was incomprehensible. Essentially, the judgment confirmed that the radio station had infringed my father's copyright, and because of that, it did not infringe on the copyright and so it did not have to pay.

Given that this judge was later dishonourably fired from the court, I would not be surprised if she had been driven by more than her misunderstanding of the law when she awarded the case to the radio station. Yes, that's another way of saying that I think they bought the judge.

I remember this as if it was yesterday. I was sitting in my room with that decision in my hands, feeling horrible. My dad came in my room and asked, *"So what are you going to do now?"*

I muttered, *"I really have no idea. I've done all that I thought needed to be done and I don't know how I could have done it any better."* He looked at me and said, *"We both know that we are in the right. We both know you did a good job. If you're not going to appeal this, you should just quit law school and find yourself another profession."*

We filed an appeal—which we lost, but at that point I refused to give up. We appealed the case even higher and it eventually made its way all the way up to the court just below the Supreme Court of Russia—this time I won. This was the best legal education I've ever received in my life.

Since that very first case, I have been hooked on intellectual property law.

During the two years it took me to win this first case, I learned so much about copyright and became so passionate about it that when my university offered me the opportunity to stay for another three years and do my PhD in law, I said that I would only be interested in doing it if I was allowed to write my dissertation on issues of intellectual property. I used that dissertation, which covered all international treaties in the field of IP, as the basis for my first book, *International Protection of Intellectual Property.*

Just shortly out of law school, I was made the CEO of a music publishing company founded by my father, mother, and myself on one side, and a recording company on the other side. It was a recording company that we had caught selling unauthorized copies of my dad's greatest hits. In the process of forcing them to pay, my dad and the recording company's president became the best of friends.

I had zero experience in running a business, and the business was crawling, but I was also the one who was responsible for drafting all sorts of agreements with authors and users of their work, so it was a priceless experience—both on the drafting and litigation side. When the global markets collapsed in 1998, we could no longer collect royalties because users had more important things to do, such as saving their own skin. I decided that the best thing to do was to dissolve the music publishing company for lack of capital or cash flow. This was one of the dumbest things I've ever done in my life, and I've blamed myself for it mercilessly for many years. If I had known what I was doing and persevered, the passive income it would be generating today would have been enormous.

In 2003, nine years into practice, I joined the Moscow office of Baker & McKenzie, the largest international law firm on the planet. This was the first time I had to work in a real law office. The firm principals and I both had our doubts about whether I'd be able to work in a large firm environment. I had to buy my very first suit and tie. I even had to cut my hair. I still keep my cut-off ponytail along with before and after photographs in my office. To my amazement and to the amazement of everyone at B&M, a glove could not have fit any better. I soon became the go-to person for all matters involving copyright and domain names.

While I was working for Baker & McKenzie, I used to take the quality of work I was involved in for granted. Now that I think about it, this is where the bulk of my diverse experience in IP came from. When I had to compile a list of my former clients and representative matters for my firm's website several years ago, I was so impressed with the list that I called my former IP principal in Moscow to thank him for the opportunity to work on those files. Indeed, I have helped hundreds of creators and businesses, including composers; designers; book writers, such as J.K. Rowling; film directors; singers; artists; individual software developers; movie producers; film companies ranging from small ones to Dreamworks; software companies ranging from one-man startups to Apple, Microsoft, and Sun; recording companies; electronics manufacturers, including Sony and Motorola; car companies, such as Porsche and Ford; apparel companies, such as Columbia Sportswear; perfumery and skincare companies, such as Amway, L'Oreal, and Mary Kay; and a countless number of other clients, big and small.

In 2006, my wife Emilia, our then six-month-old daughter, and

I went on a brief vacation to Prague. We were blown away by how quickly the Czech Republic had developed into a civilized country after the era of Soviet serfdom. Despite twenty years of transformative changes, Russia was nowhere near achieving the same result, and it wasn't even moving in that direction.

I caught my first thought, "How can some godforsaken tiny strip of land now live like a normal country, while the allegedly great Russian empire is still a very hostile place to be?" Immediately, a new thought followed, that the greatness of a country is not measured in the number of millions of people killed in various wars to protect its territory, its minerals, oil, theatres and museums; it is about whether people treat each other like decent human beings instead of a means to a collective end.

Once we realized this, we decided that we had to get out of Russia, and that it was probably our last opportunity to actually do it. For years after my first trip outside of Russia (which happened to be to the United States), I had dreamed of living there, but I was too afraid to make the move. The more successful my career became in Russia, the harder it was for me to face the reality that I would need to start over from scratch in a new country. After the Prague visit, I said to myself, *"If I don't do it now, I will never be able to do it, and I will always regret that I never even tried."*

Out of all the countries where English is an official language (which was a necessary condition if I wanted to re-launch my legal career in a new country), Canada offered the most transparent immigration system. So the decision was made.

Everyone seemed to be using my father's music, so I continued to help him protect and defend his copyrights. In fact, by the time I left Russia, there was not a single federal TV channel in Russia that I had not sued for infringing my dad's copyrights. I won every time, and I only had to do it once per channel. Subsequently, all that was necessary was for me to pick up the phone and say, "*We got you again, here's the bill.*"

When I shared my idea of moving to Canada with the then managing partner at Baker & McKenzie, who is a Canadian, she asked me, "*Do you know that you would need to go back to law school?*" At first, I thought it was a joke meant to make me stay. Then I realized that she was not kidding. She suggested that I apply to Canadian law schools from Russia. This was priceless advice that I will be forever grateful for.

In 2007, we landed in Vancouver airport, and a new chapter of my life began.

I made myself a promise to be open-minded towards other areas of law while at Canadian law school. I wanted to make sure that my focus on intellectual property was not merely an accident. No such luck. While my marks were great all around (in fact, during my last year I finished first in class in half my courses and in the top 10 in the remaining ones— not bad for an ESL student), the only times my eyes lit up were when the subject had to do with IP.

I left Russia because I am passionate about freedom, entrepreneurship, and intellectual property. Russia is a place that has never known true freedom, has had a very short period of free entrepreneurship, and has an awful record when it comes to intellectual property. This is why my mission to help business owners protect their intellectual property is so important to me.

I've always had ambitious goals and equally compelling excuses why those goals could not be achieved. I would blame a lack of public respect for intellectual property, a despotic regime in Russia, stupid judges, inadequate court awards for infringement of copyright, corrupt lawmakers, and corrupt law enforcement officials. When I caught myself on the verge of complaining about the same problems in Canada and in the world at large, I realized that while these issues may really be the cause of the world's predicament, I could no longer let my happiness remain hostage to such issues. Just because Russia (or Canada) has idiotic copyright laws does not mean that I cannot help creators protect their rights. Just as it does not mean that I should passively await the miraculous moment when everything somehow fixes itself.

In 2011, after three more years of law school and a year of articling with a Canadian law firm, the Law Society of British Columbia graciously allowed me to call myself a lawyer again. What was missing was a long line-up of law firms competing with each other for the opportunity to make me an offer of employment. Let me rephrase that, nobody wanted to hire me. I kept thinking about the line from the first Rambo movie when he said, "Back there I could fly a gunship, I could drive a tank, I was in charge of million-dollar equipment, back here I can't even hold a job parking cars!"

Right about that time, I came across Robert Kiyosaki's book *Rich Dad, Poor Dad*, where he convincingly demonstrated the difference between the insecurity of employment income and the unlimited potential of running one's own business.

This also made me remember one of the posters for my favourite band, W.A.S.P. that I've had on my wall for years. It was a picture of Blackie Lawless holding a *"Who Dares Wins"* sign. Indeed, it is amazing how easily most of us give up our childhood dreams, how easily we put up with people around us providing all the right reasons why we should take an easy road lest we fail.

It wasn't until then that I realized that I didn't fail as the CEO of the music publishing company because I was no good at being an entrepreneur. I failed because I didn't have a slightest clue how to run a company. Thinking back, I would have been a miracle if, in fact, the entire thing worked out!

So, I took a leap of faith and started my own law firm in 2011. I couldn't think of a better name, so I called it simply—Mincov Law Corporation. Very soon I discovered that not being hired by other firms was a blessing in disguise, because it allowed me to do what I love to do best—practice law in the field of intellectual property and grow everyday by learning how to be an entrepreneur. I can honestly say that the last few years have been the most exciting years of my life.

I kept looking for ways to grow my business in a way that would make the competition irrelevant. Through endless marketing trials and errors, my firm was slowly but surely gaining popularity among Canadian startups.

Remember the movie *Back to the Future*, where Dr. Emmett Brown exclaims, "I finally invented something that works!"? This is how I felt in 2013 when I came up with the idea of the Trademark Factory®, a service that provides a one-of-a-kind way to register trademarks. This was a game changer, not only because it crystallizes the unique selling proposition of my firm, but also because it allowed me to fuse all the different things I like doing into a single activity. I protect intellectual property, I run a business, I deal with brilliant people, I speak a foreign language, and I write computer code that works!

In 2015, I sacrificed my Canadian lawyer license in order to be able to deliver guaranteed flat-fee trademarking services to clients around the world. Because of many arbitrary regulations, I simply could not do what my clients wanted me to do while remaining a lawyer. Thus, I voluntarily gave up my lawyer license, renamed my firm to Trademark Factory International Inc., and our sole focus as a business is now trademarking.

Why should you care about any of this?

Because if you become my client, it won't be because IP happens to be the only way I can make a living. It will be because I deeply care about intellectual property and the ability of those who create it to protect their right to decide how their property should be used. This is also the reason I don't take cases when I would be required to justify deliberate unauthorized use of somebody else's works.

You see, one of the reasons I love doing what I do so much is that I have the privilege of dealing with brilliant people all the time. My clients create what millions of people around the world want to use, listen to, play, watch, or steal. I have profound admiration for what people have created. Without the creative genius of all these individuals, our lives would have been truly miserable. I admire my clients' accomplishments and because of that, I thoroughly enjoy the moments when I realize that I came up with an outside-the-box legal solution that helps them achieve their goals.

I strongly believe that creators deserve to have a say in how their creations are used. I strongly believe that they deserve not to have their rights and property stolen from them.

These are the reasons I do what I do and this is why I love doing it!